Anonymous

Durham Almanac

Anonymous

Durham Almanac

ISBN/EAN: 9783337334604

Printed in Europe, USA, Canada, Australia, Japan

Cover: Foto ©Suzi / pixelio.de

More available books at **www.hansebooks.com**

DURHAM
ALMANAC.

MAIN BUILDING TRINITY COLLEGE.

FOR THE YEAR OF OUR LORD
1897.

The 121st Year of American Independence, Ending 4th July.

Astronomical Calculations by Prof. W. A. Gathright, Dabney's, Va.

PUBLISHED BY

N. A. RAMSEY, ... Durham, N. C.

GO TO

DURHAM

AND STOP AT THE _____

It is a

Revelation in

Hotel

Building.

The most

Luxurious

Caravansary

in the

Southern

States.

HOWELL COBB

PROPRIETOR.

HOTEL CARROLINA.

DURHAM, N. C.

POPULATION JANUARY 1, 1896, 11,700.

During the year 1896, $12,595 were expended upon the streets of the town in permanant improvements. The 10th of December will ever be a memorable day to the friends of Trinity College, as the day that $100,000 was added to the endowment fund of the College—the gift of Mr. Washington Duke. During this year (1897) we hope to have the Public Library building completed (and if we get our dues) dirt will be broken for a $150,000 public building. Our manufacturers have paid many millions of money to the government for the privilege of running their business for the past thirty years. The building is a necessity, and we believe that "Uncle Sam" is going to give it to us. The sooner the better.

REVENUE.

The following statement of Internal Revenue taxes paid by our manufacturers, is taken from the official record of the Deputy Collector, for the fiscal year ending 30th June, 1896:

1895.		1896.	
July	$46,387.96	January	$45,656.83
August	62,885.08	February	40,885.96
September	63,569.16	March	41,975.75
October	81,087.70	April	48,588.14
November	63,405.06	May	59,776.22
December	46,166.06	June	46,299.25
	Total		$646,683.17.

These figures represent the various products stamped, as follows:

Cigarettes	514,000,000
Manufactured Tobacco (pounds)	6,290,292
Cigars and Cheroots	2,618,530
Snuff (pounds)	73,500

Reliable and Satisfactory!   **Blackwell's Durham Tobacco.**

Take the SOUTHERN RAILWAY, passing through the cities of Alexandria, Charlottesville, Lynchburg, Danville, Greensboro, Reidsville, Salisbury, Columbia and Augusta, to the South and Southwest. For information, address W. A. Turk, G. P. A., Washington, D. C.

2

DURHAM ALMANAC.

CHRONOLOGICAL CYCLES AND ERAS.

Dominical Letter	C	Julian Period	6610
Epact	26	Jewish Era	5657
Golden Number	17	Era of Nabonassa	2644
Solar Cycle	2	Olympiads	2673
Roman Indication	10	Mahommedan Era	1314

THE FOUR SEASONS.

	D.	H.
Spring commences	March 20,	3 A. M.
Summer commences	June 20,	11 P. M.
Autumn commences	September 22,	2 P. M.
Winter commences	December 21,	8 A. M.

MORNING STARS.

Mercury will be Morning Star about........Feb. 15, June 15, and Oct. 9.
Venus will be Morning Star from......... April 28 to end of the year.
Jupiter will be Morning Star..Feb. 23, and from Sept. 13 to end of year.

EVENING STARS.

Mercury will be Evening Star about...Jan. 6, April 28, Aug. 26, Dec. 20.
Venus will be Evening Star till from .... Jan. 1 to April 28.
Jupiter will be Evening Star from........February 23 to September 13.

ECLIPSES.

During the year 1897 there will be two eclipses—both of the Sun.

I. *An annular eclipse of the Sun* February 1, visible in the eastern and southern part of the United States, to Mexico and Central America, the western part of South America, and the South Pacific Ocean. Visible here as a partial eclipse towards sunset, as follows: Eclipse begins 1h. 17m. P. M.; middle of eclipse 2h. 58m. P. M.; eclipse ends 4h. 56m. P. M.

II. *An annular eclipse of the Sun* July 29, visible to the greater portions of North and South America, a small part of the Pacific Ocean, the greater part of the Atlantic Ocean, and the extreme western part of Africa. Visible here as a partial eclipse, as follows: Eclipse begins 8h. 56m. A. M.; middle of eclipse 10h. 51m. A. M.; eclipse ends 0h. 41m. P. M.

TIDES.

The time of tide can readily be found for the following places by adding the hours and minutes opposite the names to the time when the Moon is South on the day to which the tide is sought. The time when the Moon is South is given in the Calendar for every day. The next tide can be found very nearly by adding 12 hours and 29 minutes to the time of the one previous.

The tides are given in local time—add 12 minutes for Eastern Standard:

	H. M.		H. M.
Boston	11 12	New York	8 13
Sandy Hook	7 29	Old Point	8 17
Baltimore	6 33	Washington City	7 44
Richmond	4 32	Hatteras Inlet	7 04
Beaufort	7 26	Bald Head	7 26
Southport	7 19	Wilmington	9 06
Charleston	7 26	Savannah	9 33

EXPORTS.

For fiscal year ending June 30, 1896.

Manufactured Tobacco (pounds) ..   74,580
Cigarettes ... ------------------------362,613,000

Besides a large quantity of leaf is bought here for export.

WAREHOUSES.

Parrish's Warehouse, Parrish, Pope & Moore, Proprietors.
Banner Warehouse, Lea, Burch & Co., Proprietors.
Farmer's Warehouse, Ferrell & Riley, Proprietors.

From the 1st October, 1895, to 1st October, 1896, they sold 6,677,540 pounds of leaf tobacco.

OUR GRADED SCHOOL.

Our graded school is unexcelled by any other in the State. There are now 801 pupils in attendance, and every department is full. It is only a question of time when the building will have to be enlarged, or else another will have to be built, for the accommodation and education of our children. Our graded school is the pride and joy our people.

BANKS.

The First National Bank.—J. S. Carr, President; Leo D. Heartt, Cashier.

The Fidelity Bank.—B. N. Duke, President; J. F. Wily, Cashier.

The Morehead Banking Company.—W. H. Willard, President; W. M. Morgan, Cashier.

Combined capital stock amounts to $450,000.

FIRE DEPARTMENT.

We have three well-equipped companies—two white and one colored. Each company has twenty men. W. C. Bradsher, Chief; H. E. Heartt, Assistant Chief.

Water supply from a reservoir of 3,000,000 gallons capacity, 3¼ miles northwest of the city, and at an elevation of 178 feet.

The Gamewell Fire Alarm System is used.

1st Month.   JANUARY, 1897.   31 Days.

Moon's Phases.

	D. H. M.		D. H. M.
New Moon	3 0 55 a. m.	Full Moon,	18 3 8 p. m.
First Quarter,	10 4 37 p. m.	Last Quarter.	25 3 0 p. m.

Day of Month.	Day of Week.	Sun rises.	Sun sets.	Sun slow.	Sun's decline south.	ASPECTS OF PLANETS AND OTHER MISCELLANEOUS MATTER.	Moon's place.	Moon rises or sets.	Moon south.	High tides.
1	Fri	7 10	4 58	4 22	57	Negro Emancipation.		5 52	m'rn	morn
2	Sat	7 10	5 0	4 22	52	Battle of Trenton 1777.		6 55	11 33	6 37
First Sunday.						Day's length 9 hours 51 minutes.				
3	C.	7 10	5 1	5 22	46	Bat. Princeton 1777.		sets.	0 33	7 27
4	Mo	7 10	5 1	5 22	39	Vanderbilt d. 1877.		6 55	1 28	8 16
5	Tue	7 10	5 2	6 22	32	Ch. Jus. R. M. Pearson d.		7 42	2 18	9 2
6	We	7 9	5 3	6 22	25	☿ gr. Elon. E. [1878.		8 48	3 4	9 47
7	Thu	7 9	5 4	7 22	17	1st St. House burnt 1791		9 52	3 47	10 30
8	Fri	7 9	5 5	7 22	9	Forsyth Co. form'd 1848		10 48	4 28	11 14
9	Sat	7 9	5 6	8 22	0	Legislature met 1895.		11 47	5 8	11 58
Second Sunday.						Day's length 9 hours 57 minutes.				
10	C.	7 9	5 6	8 21	51	Stamp act pas'd 1765		m'rn	5 49	0 37
11	Mo	7 9	5 7	8 21	42	First Gov. N.C. 1664.		0 46	6 32	1 28
12	Tue	7 9	5 8	9 21	32	W. T. Blackwell b. 1839		1 46	7 16	2 21
13	We	7 9	5 9	9 21	22	☿ sta. Fox died 1681.		2 45	8 4	3 14
14	Thu	7 9	5 10	9 21	11	☿ in Perihelion.		3 43	8 55	4 3
15	Fri	7 9	5 11	10 21	0	Andrew Jackson b. 1767		4 40	9 49	4 51
16	Sat	7 8	5 12	10 20	48	Gibbon d. 1794.		5 36	10 44	5 36
Third Sunday.						Day's length 10 hours 5 minutes.				
17	C.	7 8	5 13	10 20	36	Dr. Franklin b. 1706		6 25	11 39	6 20
18	Mo	7 8	5 14	11 20	24	Gov. Jarvis b. 1836.		rises.	m'rn	7 1
19	Tue	7 8	5 15	11 20	11	GEN. LEE'S BIRTHDAY.		6 14	0 31	7 41
20	We	7 7	5 15	11 19	58	John Howard d. 1790.		7 23	1 22	8 23
21	Thu	7 7	5 16	12 19	44	☾ ☉ Gov. Bragg d. 1872		8 33	2 11	9 6
22	Fri	7 6	5 17	12 19	31	☿ ☉ sup. Bacon b. 1561		9 40	2 59	9 49
23	Sat	7 6	5 18	12 19	16	Wm. Gaston d. 1844.		10 48	3 46	10 36
Fourth Sunday.						Day's length 10 hours 14 minutes.				
24	C.	7 5	5 19	12 19	2	☿ gr. Hel. Lat. N.		m'rn	4 35	11 26
25	Mo	7 4	5 20	13 18	47	Fayettev'le set. 1749		0 2	5 26	0 11
26	Tue	7 3	5 21	13 18	32	Battle of Newbern 1864		1 16	6 20	1 20
27	We	7 2	5 22	13 18	16	Dr. Caldwell d. 1838.		2 29	7 18	2 21
28	Thu	7 2	5 23	13 18	0	Tripple Alliance 1667.		3 39	8 18	3 28
29	Fri	7 2	5 23	13 17	44	Kansas admitted 1861.		4 43	9 20	4 31
30	Sat	7 1	5 24	14 17	27	Charles I beheaded 1647.		5 38	10 20	5 29
Fifth Sunday.						Day's length 10 hours 28 minutes.				
31	C.	7 0	5 25	14 17	10			6 23	11 16	6 22

POST OFFICE.

W. T. Blackwell, Postmaster.

Stamps sold for fiscal year ending 30th
June, 1896_____$13,833.82
Rent for lock boxes _____ 326.15

Total revenue_____$14,159.97

SCHOOL CHILDREN.

There are, within the corporate limits of the town, children between 6 and 21 years of age: white, 1,029; colored, 367. of the white, 801 attend their graded school; of the colored, 319 attend their graded school. This shows 228 white children in our midst who are not enjoying the blessings of our school, while only 48 of the colored see fit to deny themselves of the privileges offered them. What's the matter with our white folks? This state of affairs ought not to exist. Is there no pride or love left for the 228 white children, who are thus so shamefully neglected?

REAL ESTATE, ETC.

Assessed value for 1896.

Real estate—city_____	$1,552,192	
Personal property—city_____	3,640,551	
Total_____		$ 5,192,743.00
Real estate—county_____	$1,702 419	
Personal property—county_____	596,836	
Total _____		$ 2.299,255 00
Total city and county _____		$ 7,491,998.00
Railroad taxable property_____		443,432.12
		$ 7,935,430.12

From this statement it will be seen that the town of Durham owns over 69 per cent. of the entire property of the county, and so pays over 69 per cent of the taxes.

Reliable and Satisfactory!   **Blackwell's Durham Tobacco.**

2d Month.   FEBRUARY, 1897.   28 Days.

Moon's Phases.

	D. H. M.		D. H. M.
New Moon,	1 3 5 p.m.	Full Moon,	17 5 3 a.m.
First Quarter,	9 2 17 p.m.	Last Quarter,	23 10 35 p.m.

Day of Month.	Day of Week.	Sun sets.	Sun sets.	Sun slow.	Sun's decline south.	ASPECTS OF PLANETS AND OTHER MISCELLANEOUS MATTER.	Moon's Place.	Moon rises or sets	Moon south.	High tides.
1	Mo	7 1	5 29	14 16	53	AN. ECLIPSE OF SUN.	♌	sets.	eve.	m'rn
2	Tue	7 1	5 30	14 16	36	sta. Pe'ce Conf '65	♌	6 30	0 55	7 58
3	We	7 0	5 31	14 16	18	Gen. R. Barringer d. 1895.	♐	7 36	1 40	8 41
4	Thu	6 59	5 32	14 16	0	Galvani died 1770.	♐	8 34	2 22	9 21
5	Fri	6 58	5 33	14 15	42		♒	9 34	3 3	10 0
6	Sat	6 58	5 34	14 15	23	J. J. Daniel d. 1848.	♒	10 34	3 44	10 36

First Sunday.   Day's length 10 hours 37 minutes.

7	C.	6 57	5 34	14 15	4	J. A. Womack d. 1896.	♒	11 34	4 26	11 11
8	Mo	6 56	5 35	14 14	45	Bat. Roanoke Isla'd 1862	♓	m'rn	5 9	11 48
9	Tue	6 55	5 36	14 14	26	Gen. Hancock d. '86.	♈	0 33	5 56	0 29
10	We	6 54	5 37	14 14	6	Robt. Strange d. '54.	♈	1 31	6 45	1 31
11	Thu	6 53	5 38	14 13	46	Gov. Caldwell d. 1874.	♈	2 28	7 37	2 28
12	Fri	6 53	5 39	14 13	26	H. Seymour d. 1886.	♉	3 24	8 31	3 24
13	Sat	6 52	5 40	14 13	6	Univ N. C. opened 1795	♊	4 15	9 25	4 17

Second Sunday.   Day's length 10 hours 50 minutes.

14	C.	6 51	5 41	14 12	46	ST. VALENTINE'S DAY.	♊	5 2	10 19	5 6
15	Mo	6 50	5 42	14 12	25	☿ gr. Elon. W.	♋	5 43	11 11	5 52
16	Tue	6 49	5 43	14 12	4	Judge Battle buried 1879	♋	rises.	m'rn	6 36
17	We	6 48	5 44	14 11	43	☽ ☿ in ♓.	♌	6 15	0 2	7 18
18	Thu	6 47	5 45	14 11	22	Trin. Col. chart. 1852	♌	7 28	0 51	8 0
19	Fri	6 46	5 46	15 11	0	♂ ☿ H. Vaughan d. '86	♎	8 35	1 40	8 43
20	Sat	6 45	5 47	14 10	39	Bat. of Olista, Fla., 1864	♎	9 49	2 30	9 26

Third Sunday.   Day's length 11 hours 5 minutes.

21	C.	6 43	5 48	14 10	17	Gov. Clark d. 1874.	♏	11 5	3 21	10 13
22	Mo	6 42	5 48	14 9	55	WASHINGTON b. 1732	♐	m'rn	4 16	11 3
23	Tue	6 41	5 48	13 9	33	Geo. Davis d. 1896.	♐	0 20	5 13	0 1
24	We	6 40	5 49	13 9	11	Monterey surrend'd 1846	♑	1 31	6 13	0 53
25	Thu	6 39	5 50	13 8	49	Battle of Montreal 1775.	♑	2 36	7 13	2 0
26	Fri	6 38	5 51	13 8	26	Peace Inst. estab. 1872.	♒	3 33	8 13	3 9
27	Sat	6 37	5 52	13 8	3	Bat. Moore's Creek 1776.	♒	4 20	9 9	4 13

Fourth Sunday.   Day's length 11 hours 17 minutes.

28	C.	6 36	5 53	13 7	41	Durham Co. est. 1881.	♓	4 58	10 1	5 13

DURHAM ALMANAC. 7

CITY TAXES.

For city purposes—50 cents on $100 valuation.
For graded schools—18 cents on $100 valuation.
For D. & N. R. R. bonds—12 cents on $100 valuation.
For O. & C. R. R. bonds—6 cents on $100 valuation.
For school bonds—5 cents on $100 valuation.
Making a total of 91 cents on $100 valuation.
Poll tax—$2.55.

STATE AND COUNTY TAXES.

For county—20 cents on $100 valuation.
For State—21⅔ cents on $100 valuation.
For schools—18 cents on $100 valuation.
For pensions—3½ cents on $100 valuation.
For court-house—3 cents on $100 valuation.
For R. R. bonds—5 cents on $100 valuation.
For county roads—8 cents on $100 valuation.
Making a total of 79 cents on $100 valuation.
Poll tax $2.00.

CITY INDEBTEDNESS.

For D. & N. R. R. bonds .... $ 100,000
For O. & C. R. R. bonds 50,000
For graded school bonds 24,000

Total .... $ 174,000

COUNTY INDEBTEDNESS.

For L. & D. R. R. bonds .... $ 60,000.00
For Court House 7,000.00

Total .... $ 67,000.00

STATE INDEBTEDNESS.

Four per cent. consolidated bonds .... $ 3,360,700
Six per cent. N. C. R. R. construction bonds..... 2,720,000

Total .... $ 6,080,700
The annual income to the State from its stock in
the N. C. R. R. was, under old lease ....$ 180,000
Is to be for 6 years under new lease 195,000
Is to be for 94 years under new lease 210,000

S   DURHAM ALMANAC.

3d Month.   **MARCH, 1897.**   **31 Days.**

Moon's Phases.

	D. H. M.		D. H. M.
New Moon,	3 6 48 a.m.	Full Moon,	18 4 19 p.m.
First Quarter,	11 10 20 a.m.	Last Quarter,	25 6 51 a.m.

Day of Month.	Day of Week.	Sun rises.	Sun sets.	Sun slow.	Sun's decline south.	ASPECTS OF PLANETS AND OTHER MISCELLANEOUS MATTER.	Moon's place.	Moon rises or sets.	Moon south.	High tides.
1	Mo	6 34	5 55	12	7 18	Fair and frosty.	♌	5 30	m'rn	m'rn
2	Tue	6 32	5 56	12	6 55	SHROVE TUESDAY.	♌	5 57	11 35	6 53
3	We	6 30	5 57	12	6 32	ASH WEDNESDAY.	♍	sets.	0 17	7 37
4	Thu	6 28	5 58	12	6 9	Look out for storms.	♍	7 20	0 58	8 16
5	Fri	6 26	6 0	12	5 46	Addison born 1750.	♒	8 21	1 39	8 52
6	Sat	6 24	6 0	11	5 22	Asa Biggs d. 1878.	♒	9 21	2 21	9 25

First Sunday.   Day's length 11 hours 38 minutes.

7	C.	6 23	6 1	11	4 59	Univ. N. C. estab. 1789.	♐	10 21	3 4	9 56
8	Mo	6 22	6 1	11	4 36	William III d. 1703.	♐	11 20	3 49	10 27
9	Tue	6 20	6 2	11	4 12	Battle Vera Cruz 1847.		m'rn	4 37	11 0
10	We	6 18	6 3	10	3 49	Bat. Manas. Junc. '63	♑	0 17	5 27	11 43
11	Thu	6 17	6 4	10	3 25	Wm. Barringer d. '82	♒	1 13	6 19	0 46
12	Fri	6 16	6 5	10	3 1	First Parliam't Ass. 1683.	♓	2 5	7 12	1 43
13	Sat	6 14	6 6	9	2 38	Pocahontas d. 1616.	♓	2 52	8 5	2 44

Second Sunday.   Day's length 11 hours 53 minutes.

14	C.	6 13	6 6	9	2 14	Judge Battle died 1879.	♈	3 35	8 58	3 41
15	Mo	6 12	6 7	9	1 50	Ex. sess. Leg. conv'd 1880	♈	4 12	9 48	4 35
16	Tue	6 11	6 8	9	1 27	Monroe b. 1751.	♉	4 45	10 38	5 23
17	We	6 9	6 9	8	1 3	ST. PATRICK'S DAY.	♊	5 13	11 28	6 8
18	Thu	6 8	6 10	8	0 39	Suez Canal comp. '69	♊	rises	m'rn	6 53
19	Fri	6 6	6 11	8	0 16	♀ gr. Hel. Lat. S.	♋	7 28	0 18	7 36
20	Sat	6 4	6 12	7	no'th	☉ ent. ♈, SPRING BEG.	♋	8 56	1 10	8 20

Third Sunday.   Day's length 12 hours 9 minutes.

21	C.	6 3	6 12	7	0 33	Lucknow fell 1858.	♌	10 4	2 5	9 6
22	Mo	6 2	6 13	7	0 57	J. hn C. Winder d. 1896.	♌	11 19	3 4	9 53
23	Tue	6 0	6 13	7	1 20	Battle Winchester 1862.	♍	m'rn	4 5	10 47
24	We	5 59	6 14	6	1 44	Queen Eliz'th d. 1603	♍	0 28	5 7	11 48
25	Thu	5 58	6 15	6	2 8	Thames Tun. op. 1843	♏	1 28	6 8	0 31
26	Fri	5 57	6 16	6	2 31	♀ gr. Hel. Lat. N.	♐	2 19	7 5	1 39
27	Sat	5 55	6 17	5	2 55	Bruce crowned 1306.	♐	3 0	7 59	2 48

Fourth Sunday.   Day's length 12 hours 25 minutes.

28	C.	5 53	6 18	5	3 18	Davidson Coll. op'd 1837	♑	3 32	8 47	3 53
29	Mo	5 51	6 18	5	3 41	Brit. Museum fn'd 1753.	♑	4 0	9 33	4 51
30	Tue	5 50	6 19	4	4 5	Bat. Somerville, Ky. 1863	♒	4 24	10 15	5 43
31	We	5 48	6 20	4	4 28	Mrs. M. B. Clarke d. '86	♒	4 44	10 56	6 28

DURHAM ALMANAC. 9

COUNTY OFFICIALS.

Sheriff—F. D. Markham.
Clerk of Court—W. J Christian.
Treasurer—T. J. Holloway.
Register of Deeds—W. W. Woods.
Attorney—H. A. Foushee.
Coroner—Dr. M. P. Ward.
Superintendent of Health—Dr. John M. Manning.
Jailer—John F. Howard.
Commissioners—A. D. Markham, Chairman; W. D. Turrentine, J. B. Warren.

CITY OFFICIALS.

Mayor—T. L. Peay.
Chief of Police—J. A. Woodall.
Street Commissioner—J. B. Christian.
Treasurer—P. Lunsford.
Tax Collector—J. R. Patton.
Clerk—G. W. Woodard.
Attorney—F. A. Green.
Aldermen—M. A. Angier, L A. Carr, W. M. Yearby, C. C. Taylor, T. H. Martin, T. J. Rigsbee, Dr. A. G. Carr.

CHURCHES.

Trinity (Methodist)—Rev. J. N. Cole, Pastor.
Main Street (Methodist)—Rev. G. A. Oglesby, Pastor.
Presbyterian—Rev. L. B. Turnbull, Pastor.
St. Phillips (Episcopal)—Rev. A. A. Pruden, Rector.
First Baptist—W. C. Tyree, Pastor.
Second Baptist—Rev. George J. Dowell, Pastor.
Christian—Rev. J. W. Wellons, Pastor.

BENEVOLENT SOCIETIES.

Durham Lodge, No. 352, A. F. & A. M.—E. T. Rollins, W. M.; J. Southgate, Secretary. Meet second and fourth Tuesday nights.
Durham Royal Arch Chapter, No. 48.—C. C. Taylor, H. P.; J. Southgate, Secretary. Meet third Tuesday nights.

10   DURHAM ALMANAC.

4th Month.   APRIL, 1897.   30 Days.

Moon's Phases.

	D. M. H.		D. M. H.
New Moon,	1 11 15p.m.	Full Moon,	17 1 17a.m.
First Quarter,	10 3 18a.m.	Last Quarter,	23 4 39p.m.

Day of Month	Day of Week	Sun rises	Sun sets	Sun slow	Sun's decline north	ASPECTS OF PLANETS AND OTHER MISCELLANEOUS MATTER.	Moon's place	Moon rises or sets	Moon south	High tides
1	Thu	5 47	6 22	4	4 51	ALL FOOLS DAY.		5 12	eve.	m'rn
2	Fri	5 46	6 23	3	5 14	Richmond sur. 1865		sets.	0 18	7 47
3	Sat	5 44	6 23	3	5 37	and evacuated 1865.		8 12	1 1	8 20

First Sunday.   Day's length 12 hours 42 minutes.

4	C.	5 42	6 24	3	6 0	Gen. Harrison d. 1841.		9 11	1 45	8 51
5	Mo	5 41	6 25	3	6 23	Jefferson born 1743.		10 9	2 32	9 20
6	Tue	5 39	6 26	2	6 45	Battle of Shiloh 1862.		11 5	3 21	9 50
7	We	5 38	6 27	2	7 8	Socrates died 333 B. C.		11 58	4 12	10 25
8	Thu	5 36	6 28	2	7 30	☿ in ☾. DeMedici d.1492		m'rn	5 4	11 12
9	Fri	5 35	6 29	1	7 52	☾☿☾. Lee sur. '65.		0 46	5 56	0 5
10	Sat	5 34	6 30	1	8 14	Durham incor. 1869.		1 30	6 47	1 2

Second Sunday.   Day's length 12 hours 58 minutes.

11	C.	5 33	6 31	1	8 36	Gov. Holt died 1896.		2 9	7 37	2 3
12	Mo	5 31	6 31	1	8 58	☿ in Perihelion.		2 42	8 25	3 3
13	Tue	5 30	6 32	0	9 20	Gov. Iredell d. 1853.		3 10	9 14	4 0
14	We	5 28	6 33	0	9 42	Henry Clay in Ral. 1844.		3 37	10 3	4 52
15	Thu	5 27	6 34	10	0 3	Z. B. Vance died 1894.		4 8	10 54	5 40
16	Fri	5 26	6 34	1	10 24	GOOD FRIDAY.		4 37	11 48	6 28
17	Sat	5 24	6 35	1	10 45	Dr. Franklin d. 1790		rises.	m'rn	7 16

Third Sunday.   Day's length 13 hours 13 minutes.

18	C.	5 23	6 36	1	11 6	Luther at Worms 1521.		8 57	0 47	8 2
19	Mo	5 22	6 37	1	11 27	David S. Reid b. 1813.		10 12	1 49	8 50
20	Tue	5 21	6 38	1	11 47	Napoleon 3d born 1808.		11 19	2 53	9 42
21	We	5 20	6 39	1	12 8	Santa Anna cap. 1836.		m'rn	3 57	10 38
22	Thu	5 18	6 40	2	12 28	R. C. Badger d. 1882		0 14	4 58	11 38
23	Fri	5 17	6 41	2	12 48	Cervantes d. 1616.		0 59	5 54	0 12
24	Sat	5 15	6 41	2	13 7	Dr. McKee died 1875.		1 35	6 45	1 16

Fourth Sunday.   Day's length 13 hours 27 minutes.

25	C.	5 14	6 41	2	13 27	Dr. A. Smedes d. 1877.		2 3	7 31	2 23
26	Mo	5 13	6 43	2	13 46	♃ sta. Johnson sur. '65.		2 28	8 15	3 26
27	Tue	5 12	6 43	3	14 5	B. N. Duke b. 1855.		2 50	8 56	4 23
28	We	5 11	6 44	3	14 24	☿ gr. Elon. E.		3 16	9 36	5 16
29	Thu	5 10	6 45	3	14 43	La. ceded to U. S. 1803.		3 38	10 17	6 1
30	Fri	5 9	6 46	3	15 1	Washington inaug. 1789.		4 2	10 59	6 43

DURHAM ALMANAC. 11

Durham Commandery, No. 3, Knights Templar.—James Southgate, E. C.; C. C. Taylor, Recorder. Meet first Tuesday nights.

Durham Lodge, No. 31, K. of P.—Chas. A. Jordan, C. C.; H. B. Chamberlain, K. S. Meet every Thursday night.

Golden Link Lodge, No. 114, I. O. O. F.—F. M. Sharp, N. G.; R. N. Lea, Secretary. Meet every Monday night.

Royal Arcanum.—P. M. Briggs, Regent; J. M. Whitted, Secretary. Meet second and fourth Tuesday nights.

Ehrlich Lodge, No. 4, A. O. U. W.—H. M Smith, M. W.; J. G. Piper, Recorder. Meet first and third Tuesday nights.

BUSINESS DIRECTORY OF DURHAM.

Adams, Thomas	Shoemaker
Albezette, Lewis	Foundry
Allen, J. W	Leaf Tobacco Dealer
Angier, M. A. Co	General Store
Barbee, F. M	Grocer
Barbee, R. H	Grocer
Barbee, W. F	Grocer
Bass, H. J. & Co	Leaf Tobacco Dealers
Belvin, O. W	Grocer
Bernstein, Mrs. F	Dry Goods and Clothing
Berry, J. H. & Co	Grocers and Confectioners
Blacknall, R. & Son	Drugs
Blackwell's Durham Tobacco Co	Smoking Tobacco
Brady, Henry	General Store
Brooks, Z. T. & Co	Leaf Tobacco Dealers
Bryan, E. L	Leaf Tobacco Dealer
Burton, R. C	Leaf Tobacco Dealer
Cameron, A. & Co	Lumber Dealers
Carlton, F. M	Grocer
Carr, L. A. & Co	Commission Merchants
Carrington, S. R	Cigar Manufacturer
Carrington, W. T	Leaf Tobacco Dealer
Cheek Furniture Co	Furniture
Christian, L. S. & Co	Lumber Dealers
Christian, T. S	Contractor and Builder
Cobb, Howell	Proprietor
Cohen, E	General Store
Cole, J. L. & Co	Dry Goods

5th Month.   MAY, 1897.   31 Days.

Moon's Phases.

	D. H. M.		D. H. M.
New Moon,	1 3 38 p.m.	Full Moon,	16 8 46 a.m.
First Quarter,	9 4 28 p.m.	Last Quarter,	23 4 26 a.m.
		New Moon,	31 7 17 a.m.

Day of Month.	Day of Week.	Sun rises.	Sun sets.	Sun fast.	Sun's de-cline north.	ASPECTS OF PLANETS AND OTHER MISCELLANEOUS MATTER.	Moon's place.	Moon rises or sets.	Moon south.	High tides.
1	Sat	5 8	6 47	3 15	19	Queen of May.		4 31	eve.	m'rn
First Sunday.						Day's length 13 hours 41 minutes.				
2	C.	5 7	6 48	3 15	37	S. H. Young died 1882.		sets.	0 29	7 50
3	Mo	5 6	6 49	3 15	54	Gov Tryon met Ass. 1765		8 58	1 17	8 19
4	Tue	5 5	6 49	3 16	12	Dr Wm. G. Hill d. 1877		9 53	2 8	8 49
5	We	5 4	6 50	3 16	29	Bat. Williamsburg 1862		10 43	2 59	9 21
6	Thu	5 3	6 51	4 16	46	Bat. Wilderness, Va., '64		11 29	3 51	10 3
7	Fri	5 2	6 51	4 17	2	M.C.Doub d. 1876		m'rn	4 41	10 52
8	Sat	5 1	6 52	4 17	18	Battle of Palo Alto 1846		0 8	5 30	11 51
Second Sunday.						Day's length 13 hours 53 minutes.				
9	C.	5 0	6 53	4 17	34	Bat.Spots'lva CH '64		0 41	6 18	0 25
10	Mo	4 59	6 54	4 17	50	Gen.Jackson d. 1863		1 10	7 4	1 23
11	Tue	4 58	6 54	4 18	5	G. E. Badger died 1866		1 37	7 52	2 24
12	We	4 57	6 55	4 18	20	Battle Raymond 1863.		2 4	8 40	3 23
13	Thu	4 56	6 56	4 18	35	Z. B. Vance b. 1830.		2 35	9 31	4 20
14	Fri	4 55	6 57	4 18	49	Battle Resaca,Ga ,1864.		3 2	10 27	5 15
15	Sat	4 54	6 58	4 19	3	Gov.Colquit Met.Hall '86		3 38	11 27	6 8
Third Sunday.						Day's length 14 hours 6 minutes.				
16	C.	4 53	6 59	4 19	17	in .		rises.	m'rn	7 0
17	Mo	4 53	7 0	4 19	31	John Penn b. 1741.		9 0	0 32	7 50
18	Tue	4 52	7 1	4 19	44	Matam'ras fell '46		10 1	1 38	8 42
19	We	4 52	7 1	4 19	57	Vicksburg defended '63.		10 53	2 42	9 34
20	Thu	4 51	7 2	4 20	9	Meckl. Dec Indep. 1775		11 33	3 48	10 28
21	Fri	4 50	7 3	4 20	21	Inf N.C. sec. 1861		m'rn	4 38	11 26
22	Sat	4 49	7 3	4 20	33	in Aphelion.		0 7	5 27	0 1
Fourth Sunday.						Day's length 14 hours 16 minutes.				
23	C.	4 48	7 4	3 20	44	Dr. T. H. Pritchard		0 31	6 12	0 31
24	Mo	4 48	7 5	3 20	55	d. 1896.		0 55	6 55	1 49
25	Tue	4 48	7 5	3 21	6	Bat Winchester,Va., '62		1 18	7 36	2 49
26	We	4 47	7 6	3 21	16	in Aph. Calvin d.1564		1 43	8 16	3 48
27	Thu	4 47	7 7	3 21	26	Ascension Day.		2 6	8 58	4 41
28	Fri	4 47	7 8	3 21	36	Noah Webster d. 1843.		2 33	9 41	5 30
29	Sat	4 46	7 9	3 21	45	Rhode Island adm. 1790.		3 3	10 26	6 11
Fifth Sunday.						Day's length 14 hours 25 minutes.				
30	C.	4 45	7 10	3 21	54	Fed. Dec. Day.		3 40	11 14	6 47
31	Mo	4 45	7 11	3 22	2	Bat. Fair Oaks 1862.		sets.	eve.	7 18

DURHAM ALMANAC. 13

Commonwealth Cotton Mfg. Co_____Knit Goods and Yarns
Darnell & Thomas _____Pianos and Organs
Davis, Mrs. B_____Dry Goods and Clothing
Draughan, A. J_____General Store
Duke, W., Sons & Co_____Smoking Tobacco and Cigarettes
Dunlop, E. C. & Co_____Plumbers
Durham Cigar Co_____Manufacturers
Durham Cotton Manufacturing Co _____Plaids
Durham Drug Co _____Drugs
Durham Electric Light Co.
Durham Exchange_____General Store
Durham Fertilizer Co _____Manufacturers
Durham Floral Nursery.
Durham Harper Medicine Co.
Durham Hosiery Co.
Durham Ice Co.
Durham Opium and Liquor Cure Co.
Durham Paper Box Co.
Durham Roller Covering Co.
Durham Soap Works.
Durham Steam Laundry.
Dwartz, H _____Grocer
Eakes, M _____Grocer and Fruits
Educator Co., The _____Publishers
Edwards, M. D _____Grocer
Ellis, Stone & Co _____Dry Goods
Enoch, B _____General Store
Erwin Cotton Mills_____Denims
Ferrell, W. L_____Leaf Tobacco Dealer
Follett, Mrs C. M. V_____Millinery
Forsyth, J. S _____Grocer
Fowler, A. T_____Grocer
Freeland, W. F. & Co_____Confectioners
Gardner, W. R_____Jeweler
Gattis & Son, T. J _____Books
Gladstein, M _____Clothiers and Grocers
Goldberg & Cohen _____Grocers
Golden Belt Hosiery Co.
Golden Belt Manufacturing Co_____Manufacturers of Bags
Goldstein, Aaron_____Grocer
Green, James T. & Bro_____Grocers

Reliable and Satisfactory !   **Blackwell's Durham Tobacco.**

6th Month.   JUNE, 1897.   . 30 Days

Moon's Phases.

		D. H. M.			D. H. M.
First Quarter,		8 1 54 a.m.	Last Quarter,		21 6 15 p.m.
Full Moon,		14 3 53 p.m.	New Moon,		29 9 47 p.m.

Day of Month.	Day of Week.	Sun rises.	Sun sets.	Sun fast.	Sun's decline north.	ASPECTS OF PLANETS AND OTHER MISCELLANEOUS MATTER.	Moon's place.	Moon rises or sets.	Moon south.	High tides.
1	Tue	4 44	7 11	2	22 10	Battle Cold Harbor 1864.		8 41	eve.	m'rn
2	We	4 44	7 12	2	22 18	U sta. Marietta taken '64		9 26	1 47	8 23
3	Thu	4 43	7 12	2	22 25	Jeff. Davis born 1808.		10 6	2 38	9 1
4	Fri	4 42	7 13	2	22 32	George I born 1738.		10 42	3 27	9 43
5	Sat	4 41	7 13	2	22 39	Telegraph in China 1871.		11 13	4 15	10 34

First Sunday.   Day's length 13 hours 33 minutes.

6	C.	4 41	7 14	2	22 45	Patrick Henry d. 1799.		11 40	5 1	11 30
7	Mo	4 41	7 14	1	22 51	Rob't Bruce d. 1329.		m'rn	5 46	0 1
8	Tue	4 41	7 15	1	22 56	Bat. Cross Keys 1862		0 4	6 33	0 47
9	We	4 41	7 15	1	23 1	Georgia chartered 1732.		0 34	7 21	1 46
10	Thu	4 41	7 16	1	23 5	State Cap. burned 1831.		1 1	8 12	2 48
11	Fri	4 41	7 16	1	23 9	Sherman at Kennesaw '64		1 31	9 9	2 52
12	Sat	4 41	7 16	0	23 13	d $ h). Bryant d. 1878.		2 11	10 10	4 55

Second Sunday.   Day's length 14 hours 35 minutes.

13	C.	4 41	7 16	slow	23 16	Gen. Scott b. 1786.		2 57	11 15	5 55
14	Mo	4 41	7 17		23 19	1st pros. by Nero 64.		rises.	m'rn	6 49
15	Tue	4 41	7 18		23 22	U gr. Elon. W.		8 40	0 21	7 42
16	We	4 41	7 18	0	23 24	John Pool born 1826.		9 26	1 25	8 33
17	Thu	4 41	7 19	1	23 25	Addison died 1719.		10 2	2 24	9 23
18	Fri	4 41	7 19	1	23 27	d h $ Bat. Waterloo 1815		10 33	3 17	10 15
19	Sat	4 42	7 19	1	23 27	Gov. Reid d. 1891.		10 57	4 6	11 5

Third Sunday.   Day's length 14 hours 36 minutes.

20	C.	4 43	7 19	1	23 28	O ent. 69. SUM. BEG		11 21	4 50	11 59
21	Mo	4 43	7 19	2	23 28	The Bi'k Hole tr. 1756		11 47	5 33	0 16
22	Tue	4 43	7 19	2	23 27	Bat. Rameeur's Mills 1780		m'rn	6 14	1 10
23	We	4 43	7 19	2	23 27	Bat. of Chickahominy '62		0 9	6 55	2 6
24	Thu	4 43	7 19	2	23 25	ST. JOHN BAPTIST.		0 35	7 38	3 5
25	Fri	4 43	7 20	2	23 24	$ in Aphelion.		1 5	8 23	4 2
26	Sat	4 44	7 20	3	23 22	d $). L. Bonaparte d. '46		1 39	9 10	4 50

Fourth Sunday.   Day's length 14 hours 36 minutes.

27	C.	4 44	7 20	3	23 19	Prof. Mitchell died 1857.		2 20	9 59	5 36
28	Mo	4 44	7 20	3	23 16	Vicksburg bomb. '62		3 5	10 50	6 13
29	Tue	4 45	7 20	3	23 13	Nat. Macon d. 1837.		3 58	11 43	6 49
30	We	4 45	7 20	3	23 9	Dr. John Manning b. '30		sets.	0 34	7 24

Greenburg, M _____ Grocer
Griswold, W. J _____ M'dse Broker and Insurance
Harden, G. M., Jr_____ Livery
Haskell, M_____ Dry Goods and Clothing
Heartt & Hackney _____ Drugs
Henry, R. L _____ Leaf Tobacco Dealer
Herald Publishing Co.
Herndon & Bagwell _____ Grocers
Hewitt, W. A_____ Grocer
Hicks, J. D _____ Grocer
Holder & Couch _____ Wood and Coal
Holland, Cary _____ Manufacturer Bed Springs
Holloway, J. A _____ Manufacturer Carriages
Holman & Co., S. W_____ Plumbers
House Furnish'g and Decorating Agency___S. F. Tomlinson
Howerton, C. P _____ Carriages
Howerton, R. T _____ Undertaker
Hulin, C. J _____ Tombstones
Hunt, S. R_____ Grocer
Jenkins & Co., Miss Minnie _____ Millinery
Jones, M. H _____ Jeweler
Jourdan, C. E _____ Grocer
Kelly, J. D_____ Grocer.
Kelly, R_____ Grocer
Kerr, J. T_____ Foundry
Kilby, V. S. & Co_____ Merchandise Broker
Kootz, Louis _____ Grocer
Kramer, A_____ Leaf Tobacco Dealer
Kramer & Co., Sam_____ Manufacturer Cigars
Lambe, T. J _____ Clothing
Leading Racket Store_____ Dry Goods and Clothing
Lee & Wheeler_____ Cabinet and Undertakers
Levy, Mrs. Carrie J_____ Dry goods and Clothing
Levy, S_____ Grocer
Lewith, A. E _____ Furniture
Lloyd, A. E., & Co _____ Hardware
Lougee, Geo. E._____ Tinner
Lyon & Co. Tobacco Works_____ M'frs Smoking Tobacco
McCabe, W. H_____ Insurance
McCollum & Co_____ Grocers
McCown, M. E._____ Livery

Reliable and Satisfactory! **Blackwell's Durham Tobacco.**

Take the SOUTHERN RAILWAY, passing through the cities of Alexandria, Charlottesville, Lynchburg, Danville, Greensboro, Reidsville, Salisbury, Columbia and Augusta, to the South and Southwest. For information, address W. A. Turk, G. P. A., Washington, D. C.

7th Month. JULY, 1897. 31 Days.

Moon's Phases.

	D.	H.	M.		D.	H.	M.
☽ First Quarter,	7	8	24 a.m.	☾ Last Quarter,	21	10	0 a.m
Full Moon,	13	11	44 p.m.	New Moon,	29	10	49 a.m

Day of Month.	Day of Week.	Sun rises.	Sun sets.	Sun slow.	Sun's decline north.	ASPECTS OF PLANETS AND OTHER MISCELLANEOUS MATTER.	Moon's place.	Moon rises or sets.	Moon south.	High Tides.
1	Thu	4 45	7 20	4	23 5	⊕ in Aphelion.	♋	8 43	eve.	m'rn
2	Fri	4 46	7 20	4	23 1	Garfield assassin't'd 1881	♋	9 16	2 13	8 42
3	Sat	4 47	7 20	4	22 56	☌♂☽. Prov. 12:2.	♋	9 43	2 59	9 26
First Sunday.						Day's length 14 hours 33 minutes.				
4	C.	4 47	7 20	4	22 50	☌♃☽. INDE. DAY 1776.	♌	10 8	3 45	10 14
5	Mo	4 48	7 19	4	22 45	☿ in ♌. Monroe d. 1831.	♌	10 36	4 30	11 4
6	Tue	4 48	7 19	5	22 38	☽ Hamlin d. 1891.	♍	11 5	5 17	11 59
7	We	4 49	7 19	5	22 32	♀ gr. Elon. W.	♍	11 32	6 6	0 15
8	Thu	4 50	7 19	5	22 25	Vicksburg cap. 1863.	♍	m'rn	6 58	1 13
9	Fri	4 50	7 19	5	22 18	Judge M E Manly d. 1881	♎	0 6	7 56	2 20
10	Sat	4 51	7 18	5	22 10	☌ ♄ ⛢ ☽.	♎	0 49	8 57	3 32
Second Sunday.						Day's length 14 hours 26 minutes.				
11	C.	4 52	7 18	5	22 2	J. Q. Adams b. 1767.	♏	3 39	10 2	4 40
12	Mo	4 52	7 18	5	21 54	Bat. of Bayou 1690.	♏	2 41	11 6	5 43
13	Tue	4 53	7 17	6	21 45	Gen. Fremont d. 1890	♐	rises.	m'rn	6 40
14	We	4 53	7 17	6	21 36	Peace Cong. London 1890	♐	7 57	0 7	7 32
15	Thu	4 54	7 16	6	21 26	☌ ☿ ⊙ superior.	♑	8 32	1 3	8 21
16	Fri	4 55	7 16	6	21 16	Mrs. Lincoln d. 1882.	♑	8 57	1 55	9 7
17	Sat	4 55	7 15	6	21 6	Gen. J. J. Pettigrew k '63.	♒	9 21	2 42	9 53
Third Sunday.						Day's length 14 hours 19 minutes.				
18	C.	4 56	7 15	6	20 55	Fan'ing cap. Pittsb'o 1781	♒	9 50	3 26	10 38
19	Mo	4 57	7 14	6	20 44	☿ gr. Hel. Lat. N.	♓	10 12	4 9	11 20
20	Tue	4 57	7 13	6	20 33	Bat. Winchester Va. '64.	♓	10 36	4 51	11 59
21	We	4 58	7 13	6	20 21	☾ Bat. Bull Run 1862.	♓	11 7	5 33	0 20
22	Thu	4 59	7 12	6	20 9	Chatham County	♈	11 38	6 18	1 13
23	Fri	5 0	7 12	6	19 57	[established 1770.	♈	m'rn	7 4	2 13
24	Sat	5 1	7 11	6	19 44	Bolivar b. 1783.	♈	0 15	7 52	3 15
Fourth Sunday.						Day's length 14 hours 9 minutes.				
25	C.	5 2	7 11	6	19 31	Bat. Lundy's Lane 1814.	♉	1 0	8 43	4 11
26	Mo	5 3	7 10	6	19 18	Ju'ge J. E. Shepherd b. '48	♉	1 49	9 35	4 58
27	Tue	5 3	7 9	6	19 4	Cab strike in London '53.	♊	2 46	10 27	5 42
28	We	5 3	7 8	6	18 50	♄ stationary.	♊	3 47	11 19	6 21
29	Thu	5 4	7 7	6	18 36	An. ecl. of sun, visibl.	♋	sets.	ev 8	7 0
30	Fri	5 5	7 6	6	18 22	☌ ☿ ☽. Wm. Penn d. 1718	♋	7 47	0 56	7 39
31	Sat	5 6	7 6	6	18 7	Andrew Johnson d. 1875	♌	8 13	1 43	8 20

BLACKWELL'S DURHAM TOBACCO is the most honest, popular, uniform, reliable, satisfactory Smoking Tobacco ever put upon the market, hence dealers and consumers always pronounce it "THE BEST."

Mallory Durham Cheroot Co .... Manufacturers Cigars
Mangum, B. W .... Grocer
Mangum, W., & Son .... General Store
Markham, H. H .... General Store
Martin, T. H .... Leaf Tobacco Dealer
Max, A .... General Store
Mesley, J. S .... Merchant Tailor
Miller, M., & Co .... Grocers
Morris, R. F., & Sons Mfg. Co ... Mfrs. Snuff and Smo. Tobacco
Murray, J. G .... Sewing Machines
Newton, W. S .... Leaf Tobacco Dealer
Norris, W. J .... Grocer
Norton, C. H .... Contractor and Builder
O'Briant, P. P .... Builder
Owen, B. F .... Grocer
Owen, J. E., & Co .... Grocers
Patterson, E. O .... Grocer
Pearl Cotton Mills .... Manufacturers Cotton Warps
Peay, Thos. L .... Leaf Tobacco Dealer
Perry, S. R .... Leaf Tobacco Dealer
Perry, D. W., & Son .... Grocers
Pinnix, J. T., & Co .... Leaf Tobacco Dealers
Postley, C. T .... Jeweler
Pridgen & Jones .... Boots and Shoes
Proctor, W. H .... Grocer
Ramsey, N. A .... Publisher Durham Almanac
Rawls, Q. E .... Dry Goods and Notions
Rawls Brothers .... Dry Goods and Notions
Reams, I. M .... Leaf Tobacco Dealer
Rigsbee, A. M .... Grocer
Robinson, J. A .... Editor "Sun"
Rosemond & Co., H. M .... Grocers and Confectioners
Rowland & Cooper .... Leaf Tobacco Dealers
Royal & Borden .... Furniture
Sears, A. A .... Livery
Seeman Carriage Co .... Manufacturers
Separk, W. D .... Upholsterer
Shelburn, Wm .... Photographer
Slade, W. T .... Grocer
Slater Co., W. A .... Clothing
Smith, Mrs. Ada M .... Millinery

8th Month. AUGUST, 1897. 31 Days.

Moon's Phases.

	D.	H.	M.		D.	H.	M.
First Quarter,	5	1	16p.m.	Last Quarter,	20	3	21a.m.
Full Moon,	12	9	14a.m.	New Moon,	27	10	21p.m.

Day of Month.	Day of Week.	Sun rises.	Sun sets.	Sun slow.	Sun's decline north.	ASPECTS OF PLANETS AND OTHER MISCELLANEOUS MATTER.	Moon's place.	Moon rises or sets.	Moon south.	High Tides.
First Sunday.						Day's length 13 hours 59 minutes.				
1	C.	5 6	7 5	6	17 52	☌♃☽. George II cr. 1714.		8 41	eve.	m'rn
2	Mo	5 7	7 4	6	17 36	♅ sta.		9 9	3 15	9 53
3	Tue	5 8	7 3	6	17 20	Columbus left Spain 1492		9 35	4 3	10 43
4	We	5 9	7 2	6	17 4	J. C. Dobbin d. 1857.		10 7	4 54	11 25
5	Thu	5 10	7 1	6	16 48	Battle Athens 1861.		10 46	5 49	0 1
6	Fri	5 11	7 1	6	16 31	☌♄☽. Ft Gains sur. 1864		11 33	6 48	1 0
7	Sat	5 11	7 0	6	16 15	Barzelius d. 1848.		m'rn	7 50	2 0
Second Sunday.						Day's length 13 hours 46 minutes.				
8	C.	5 12	6 58	5	15 57	Judge J. J. Davis d. 1892		0 29	8 52	3 16
9	Mo	5 13	6 56	5	15 40	Gov. Graham d. 1875.		1 33	9 53	4 28
10	Tue	5 14	6 55	5	15 22	Battle Oak Hill 1861.		2 43	10 50	5 31
11	We	5 14	6 54	5	15 5	Gov. Graham d. 1875		3 55	11 43	6 27
12	Thu	5 15	6 53	5	14 47	☿ in ☊. R. E. Lee d. '70		rises.	m'rn	7 16
13	Fri	5 16	6 52	5	14 28	☌☿♃. Conova d. 1822.		7 23	0 32	8 0
14	Sat	5 17	6 51	4	14 10	Battle of Hastings 1066.		7 50	1 18	8 43
Third Sunday.						Day's length 13 hours 32 minutes.				
15	C.	5 18	6 50	4	13 51	Napoleon b. 1769.		8 16	2 2	9 25
16	Mo	5 19	6 49	4	13 32	Napoleon at Helena 1815		8 38	2 45	10 7
17	Tue	5 19	6 48	4	13 13	Snr. of Burgoyne 1777.		9 4	3 27	10 49
18	We	5 20	6 46	4	12 53	G. W. Watts b. 1851.		9 36	4 11	11 20
19	Thu	5 21	6 45	3	12 34	Judge W. Clark b. '46		10 12	4 57	11 58
20	Fri	5 21	6 44	3	12 14	Benj. Harrison b. '33		10 53	5 45	0 23
21	Sat	5 22	6 43	3	11 54	Bat. of Ball's Bluff 1861.		11 41	6 34	1 8
Fourth Sunday.						Day's length 13 hours 19 minutes.				
22	C.	5 23	6 42	3	11 33	☿ in Aphe. Gough b. '17		m'rn	7 26	2 18
23	Mo	5 24	6 40	2	11 13	Com. Perry d. 1820.		0 34	8 18	3 23
24	Tue	5 25	6 39	2	10 52	☌♀☽. D. Webster d. '52		1 32	9 9	4 19
25	We	5 26	6 38	2	10 32			2 35	10 0	5 9
26	Thu	5 27	6 36	2	10 11	☿ gr. Elon. E.		3 39	10 49	5 51
27	Fri	5 27	6 35	1	9 50	Gov. Swain d. 1868.		4 45	11 36	6 33
28	Sat	5 28	6 33	1	9 28	☌♃☽. 1st Cable Mes. 1858		sets.	0 24	7 17
Fifth Sunday,						Day's length 13 hours 4 minutes.				
29	C.	5 28	6 32	1	9 7	T. B. Kingsbury b. 1828.		7 13	1 11	8 0
30	Mo	5 29	6 31	0	8 45	☌☿☽. Wm. Penn d. 1718.		7 40	2 0	8 44
31	Tue	5 30	6 30	0	8 24	Earthquake 1886.		8 10	2 51	9 32

DURHAM ALMANAC. 19

Smith, J. W	Leaf Tobacco Dealer
Smith, P. S	Grocer
Smoot, W. H	Leaf Tobacco Dealer
Sneed, Paul J	Drugs
Southgate & Son, J	Insurance
Stroud, T. E	Sewing Machines
Stroud, W. D	Grocer
Sullivan, J. H	Grocer
Summerfield & Co., C	Clothing
Surles W. B	Merchandise Broker
Tatum, J. W	Grocer
Taylor, C. C	Stoves and Tinware
Thaxton, Mrs. Nora B	Grocer
Thomas & Hobgood	Photographers
Thompson, Eugene C	Grocer
Thompson, Mrs. M. F	Grocer
Umstead, A. K., & Co	Leaf Tobacco Dealers
Umstead, J. N	Leaf Tobacco Dealer
Vaughan, P. W	Drugs
Walker, J. W., Jr	Coal Dealer
Weatherspoon, W. H	Grocer
Whitley, R. D	Jeweler
Whitmore, J. L	Baker and Confectioner
Williams & Hughes	China, etc
Wills, H. C., & Co	Plumber
Womble, J. T	Hardware
Woodall, B. C. & J. A	Harness
Woods, J. H	Oils
Wortham Wooden Mills	Mfrs Sash, Doors, etc
Wyatt, J. M	Saddlery and Harness
Yearby, W. M	Drugs

"Talk about a woman's sphere, as if it had a limit!
  There's not a place in earth or heaven,
  There's not a task to mankind given,
  There's not a blessing or a woe,
  There's not a whisper, yes or no,
  There's not a life or death or birth,
  That has a feather's weight of worth,
  Without a woman in it."

9th Month.   **SEPTEMBER, 1897.**   **30 Days.**

Moon's Phases.

	D.	H.	M.			D.	H.	M.
First Quarter,	3	6	5p.m.	Last Quarter,	18	9	42p.m.
Full Moon,	10	9	3p.m.	New Moon,	26	8	38a.m.

Day of Month.	Day of Week.	Sun rises.	Sun sets.	Sun fast.	Sun's decline north.	ASPECTS OF PLANETS AND OTHER MISCELLANEOUS MATTER.	Moon's place.	Moon rises or sets.	Moon south.	High Tides.
1	We	5 31	6 28		8 2	Battle of Ox Hill 1862.		8 47	eve.	m'rn
2	Thu	5 32	6 27	fast.	7 40	Atlanta cap. 1864.		9 31	4 43	11 10
3	Fri	5 33	6 25	1	7 18	Gov. Swain d. 1868.		10 23	5 43	11 57
4	Sat	5 34	6 24	1	6 56	Wm. A. Graham b. 1804		11 25	6 45	0 30

First Sunday.   Day's length 12 hours 47 minutes.

5	C.	5 35	6 22	2	6 33	Confed. invade Md. '62.		m'rn	7 45	1 48
6	Mo	5 35	6 21	2	6 11	LABOR DAY. LEG. HOL.		0 31	8 43	3 5
7	Tue	5 36	6 19	2	5 28	Castelor inaug. 1873.		1 42	9 36	4 15
8	We	5 36	6 18	3	5 26	☿ sta. Jewsle.Poland 187		2 51	10 25	5 14
9	Thu	5 37	6 16	3	5	California admitted 1850		4 0	11 12	6 7
10	Fri	5 38	6 15	3	4 40	S. S. Cox d. 1889.		5 8	11 56	6 53
11	Sat	5 39	6 14	4	4 18	☿ gr. Hel. Lat. S.		rises.	m'rn	7 36

Second Sunday.   Day's length 12 hours 33 min.

12	C.	5 39	6 12	4	3 55	Bat.of Chapultepec 1847		6 41	0 39	8 16
13	Mo	5 40	6 11	4	3 32	♂♃⊙. Bat. Quebec1750.		7 6	1 22	8 55
14	Tue	5 41	6 10	5	3 9	W. P. Mangum d. 1861.		7 35	2 5	9 33
15	We	5 42	6 8	5	2 45	Gen.Scott took Mex.1847		8 9	2 50	10 13
16	Thu	5 43	6 6	5	2 22	Farenheit d. 1737.		8 48	3 37	10 50
17	Fri	5 44	6 5	6	1 59	Mt.CenisTun.op.'71.		9 33	4 26	11 35
18	Sat	5 44	6 4	6	1 36	Fug. slave act 1850.		10 23	5 17	0 2

Third Sunday.   Day's length 12 hours 17 min.

19	C.	5 45	6 2	6	1 12	Garfield d. 1881.		11 19	6 8	0 30
20	Mo	5 45	6 1	7	0 49	Arthur inaugura'd 1881		m'rn	6 59	1 25
21	Tue	5 46	6 0	7	0 26	Bat. of Fisher's Hill 1864		0 18	7 49	2 40
22	We	5 47	5 58	7	0 2	⊙ ent. ♎. AUTUMN BEG.		1 21	8 38	3 41
23	Thu	5 48	5 56	8	so'th	Russian fleet sank 1854.		2 26	9 26	4 34
24	Fri	5 49	5 54	8	0 46	Gen. D. H. Hill d. 1889.		3 34	10 13	5 21
25	Sat	5 50	5 53	8	1 9	♂☿☽.Bat.Montreal1775		4 43	11 1	6 8

Fourth Sunday.   Day's length 12 hours 1 minute.

26	C.	5 51	5 52	9	1 33	Proverbs 22: 1.		5 48	11 50	6 53
27	Mo	5 51	5 50	9	1 56	Steam. Arctic lost'54		sets.	ev 42	7 39
28	Tue	5 51	5 49	9	2 19	Bishop Randall d. 1873.		6 44	1 36	8 25
29	We	5 52	5 47	10	2 43	Prov. xxvii: 1.		7 28	2 35	9 13
30	Thu	5 53	5 46	10	3 6	☿ in ☊.Whitfield d.1770		8 18	3 36	10 3

Take the SOUTHERN RAILWAY, passing through the cities of Alexandria, Charlottesville, Lynchburg, Danville, Greensboro, Reidsville, Salisbury, Columbia and Augusta, to the South and Southwest. For information, address W. A. Turk, G. P. A., Washington, D. C.

NORTH CAROLINA AS A MANUFACTURING STATE— COTTON AND WOOLEN MILLS.

```
Number of mills ------------------------------------    189
    "       "    in course of construction----------      7
    "    spindles employed----------------------888,792
    "    looms      "     ----------------------- 20,742
    "    men        "     -----------------------  6,822
    "    women      "     ----------------------- 10,567
    "    children   "   (3,379 under 14) -------  6,046
Wages per day—skilled men--------------------99 cents
   "    "    "   unskilled men----------------67   "
   "    "    "   skilled women----------------66   "
   "    "    "   unskilled women -------------47½  "
   "    "    "   children ---------------------31   "
```

RAILROAD, TELEGRAPH AND STEAMBOAT STATISTICS IN NORTH CAROLINA, 30th JUNE, 1896.

Total mail line, mileage 3,445.53, distributed and valued, as follows:

```
Southern Railway, 1,004.34 at--------------$ 8,104,960.01
Atlantic Coast Line, 686.06 at--------------  6,852,349 65
Seaboard Air Line, 613.40 at---------------  5,265,195.17
Miscellaneous Roads, 1,141.73 at----------  5,775,555.89

                                           $25,998,060.72
Pulman Cars----------------------------$    83,982.47
Telegraph Companies -------------------    215,273.80
Steamboat Companies ------------------    278,780.00

   Total valuation --------------------$26,576,096.99
```

On the various roads there are 9,417 employees. Increase in mileage for year ending 30th June, 1896, as follows:

```
   Caldwell and Northern ------------------ 10.60
   Hendersonville and Brevard------------- 21.60
   Aberdeen and West End ---------------  7.25

      Total new mileage ------------------ 39.45
```

Reliable and Satisfactory!   **Blackwell's Durham Tobacco.**

10th Month.   OCTOBER, 1897.   31 Days.

Moon's Phases.

	D. H. M.		D. H. M.
First Quarter,	3 0 23a.m.	Last Quarter,	18 4 0p.m.
Full Moon,	10 11 33a.m.	New Moon,	25 6 20p.m.

Day of Month.	Day of Week.	Sun rises.	Sun sets.	Sun fast.	Sun's decline north.	ASPECTS OF PLANETS AND OTHER MISCELLANEOUS MATTER.	Moon's place.	Moon rises or sets.	Moon south.	High Tides.
1	Fri	5 54	5 44	10	3 29			9 18	eve.	m'rn
2	Sat	5 55	5 43	11	3 53	Gen. Ass. at Edenton 1722		10 25	5 40	11 58

First Sunday.　　　　　　　　　Day's length 11 hours 45 min.

3	C.	5 56	5 41	11	4 16	Black Hawk d. 1838.		11 34	6 38	0 21
4	Mo	5 57	5 40	11	4 39	Bat. Germ'n t'wn 1777		m'rn	7 32	1 37
5	Tue	5 58	5 37	12	5 2	☿ in Perihelion.		0 42	8 22	2 52
6	We	5 59	5 35	12	5 25	W. H. Haywood d. 1852.		1 51	9 8	3 56
7	Thu	5 59	5 34	12	5 48	Bat. Kings Mount'n 1780		2 57	9 52	4 52
8	Fri	6 0	5 32	13	6 11	Bat. Fort Pickens 1861.		4 1	10 35	5 42
9	Sat	6 1	5 30	13	6 34	Gr. Fire in Chicago 1871		4 59	11 18	6 27

Second Sunday.　　　　　　　　Day's length 11 hours 27 min.

10	C.	6 2	5 29	13	6 57	Stuart raid. Pa. 1862		rises.	m'rn	7 9
11	Mo	6 3	5 28	13	7 19	Rev. W. E. Pell d. '70.		5 36	0 1	7 48
12	Tue	6 4	5 27	14	7 42	J. S. Carr b. 1845.		6 9	0 45	8 26
13	We	6 5	5 25	14	8 4	Conova d. 1822.		6 46	1 32	9 3
14	Thu	6 6	5 24	14	8 27	Bat. of Hastings 1066.		7 29	2 20	9 40
15	Fri	6 7	5 23	14	8 49	☿ gr. Hel. Lat. N.		8 16	3 10	10 19
16	Sat	6 8	5 21	14	9 11	Napoleon at Helena 1815		9 10	4 0	11 2

Third Sunday.　　　　　　　　　Day's length 11 hours 10 min.

17	C.	6 9	5 19	15	9 33	Sur. Burgoyne 1777.		10 6	4 51	11 50
18	Mo	6 9	5 18	15	9 55	Judge Reade d. 1894		11 6	5 40	0 10
19	Tue	6 10	5 17	15	10 16	Bat. Cedar Creek 1866.		m'rn	6 29	0 59
20	We	6 11	5 16	15	10 38	Grace Darling d. 1812.		0 8	7 16	2 8
21	Thu	6 12	5 15	15	10 59	Bat. of Ball's Bluff 1861.		1 13	8 2	3 9
22	Fri	6 13	5 14	15	11 20	Hon. Thos. Kenan d. 1843		2 22	8 49	4 5
23	Sat	6 14	5 12	16	11 41	Wm. Hooper d. 1790.		3 25	9 37	4 56

Fourth Sunday.　　　　　　　　Day's length 10 hours 56 min.

24	C.	6 15	5 11	16	12 2	Water Mills invent. 555.		4 38	10 27	5 45
25	Mo	6 16	5 10	16	12 23	Newbern set. 1712.		5 55	11 21	6 33
26	Tue	6 16	5 9	16	12 43	Salisb'ry l'id off 1753		sets.	0 19	7 19
27	We	6 17	5 8	16	13 4			6 8	1 21	8 8
28	Thu	6 18	5 7	16	13 24	Proverbs 28: 1.		7 6	2 26	8 57
29	Fri	6 19	5 6	16	13 44	Sir Walter Ral'gh d. 1618		8 12	3 30	9 48
30	Sat	6 20	5 5	16	14 3	Gambetta b. 1838.		9 23	4 31	10 42

Fifth Sunday.　　　　　　　　　Day's length 10 hours 44 min.

31	C.	6 21	5 5	16	14 23	♂ in ☊. Gen. Scott ret. '61		10 35	5 28	11 40

DURHAM ALMANAC. 23

GROSS EARNINGS.

Southern Railway	$3,899,727.51
Atlantic Coast Line	2,436,209.11
Seaboard Air Line	2,140,633.10
Miscellaneous Roads	1,339,549.14
	$9,816,118.86

MILEAGE AND VALUATION IN DURHAM COUNTY.

Durham and Northern	12.20 at	$ 60,451.37
North Carolina	18.69 at	210,548.98
Oxford and Clarksville	11.92 at	58,373.07
Norfolk and Western	20.64 at	114,058.70
Total	63.45	$443,432.12

BANKS WITHIN THE STATE.

There are 93 banks in North Carolina—28 National, 40 State, 19 Private, and 6 Savings. On the 6th October, 1896, they had on hand:

Gold coin	$ 541.283.50
Silver coin	146,723.22
All other currency	852,488.10
	$1,540,494.82
Total resources amount to	$19,958,763.36
Capital stock paid in	5,436,970.04
Surplus fund	1,157,014.44
Undivided profits	566,871.42
Individual deposits	9,328,956.58

[These figures taken from report of the State Treasurer.]

RAILROAD SPEED RECORD.

Engine No. 999, of the New York Central, has the speed record of the world for long as well as for short distances, having made one mile in 32 seconds, and at the rate of 112.5 miles an hour; 500 miles in 5 hours; and 646 miles in 9 hours and 58 minutes, or at the rate of 64.8 miles an hour.

11th Month. NOVEMBER, 1897. 30 Days.

Moon's Phases.

	D. H. M.		D. H. M.
First Quarter,	1 9 28a.m.	Last Quarter,	17 8 54a.m.
Full Moon,	9 4 42a.m.	New Moon,	24 4 11a.m.
		First Quarter,	30 10 6p.m.

Day of Month.	Day of Week.	Sun rises.	Sun sets.	Sun fast.	Sun's decline south.	ASPECTS OF PLANETS AND OTHER MISCELLANEOUS MATTER.	Moon's place.	Moon rises or sets.	Moon south.	High Tides.
1	Mo	6 22	5 3	16 14	42	McLellan in com. '61		11 43	eve.	m'rn
2	Tue	6 23	5 2	16 15	1			m'rn	7 7	1 21
3	We	6 24	5 1	16 15	20	Bat. of Hohenlinden 1800		1 50	7 51	2 23
4	Thu	6 25	5 0	16 15	38	Geo. Peabody d. 1869.		1 54	8 34	3 30
5	Fri	6 26	4 59	16 15	56	Gen. Grant's 2d elec.1870		2 54	9 16	4 25
6	Sat	6 27	4 58	16 16	14	♀ gr. Hel. Lat∙ N.		3 54	9 59	5 41

First Sunday. Day's length 10 hours 28 min.

7	C.	6 28	4 56	16 16	32	Dr. B. Craven d. 1882.		4 55	10 42	5 59
8	Mo	6 29	4 56	16 16	49	♂ ☿☽ superior.		5 53	11 28	6 40
9	Tue	6 30	4 55	16 17	6			rises.	m'rn	7 20
10	We	6 31	4 55	16 17	23	Martin Luther b. 1483.		5 26	0 15	7 58
11	Thu	6 32	4 54	16 17	39	Washington admit. 1889		6 12	1 5	8 34
12	Fri	6 33	4 53	16 17	56	☌ ☿ ♂.		7 3	1 55	9 11
13	Sat	6 34	4 53	16 18	12	Fall of Meteors 1833.		7 58	2 45	9 49

Second Sunday. Day's length 10 hours 17m.

14	C.	6 35	4 52	15 18	27	A. S. Merrimon d. 1892.		8 56	3 35	10 29
15	Mo	6 36	4 51	15 18	42	Bat. Campbell Sta. 1863.		9 56	4 23	11 13
16	Tue	6 37	4 51	15 18	57	Gr. fire in Durh'm '87		10 58	5 9	11 59
17	We	6 38	4 50	15 19	12	Suez Canal op. 1869.		m'rn	5 55	0 31
18	Thu	6 39	4 50	15 19	26	☿ in Aphelion.		0 2	6 39	1 35
19	Fri	6 40	4 49	14 19	40	Gen. Ass.at Newb'rn1771		1 9	7 25	2 36
20	Sat	6 41	4 49	14 19	53	Erup.of Mt Vesuvius 57.		2 12	8 12	3 36

Third Sunday. Day's length 10 hours 7 min.

21	C.	6 42	4 49	14 20	7	☌ ♂ ☉.		3 26	9 3	4 29
22	Mo	6 43	4 48	14 20	19	Gen. Jos. Graham d. 1836		4 40	9 58	5 22
23	Tue	6 44	4 47	13 20	32	Gov. Ellis b. 1820.		6 0	10 50	6 13
24	We	6 45	4 47	13 20	44	☌ ☿ ☽!		sets.	0 3	7 3
25	Thu	6 46	4 46	13 20	55	♂ ♄ ☉∙Isa'c Watts d.1748		5 51	1 10	7 53
26	Fri	6 47	4 46	12 21	7	Bishop Marvin d. 1875.		7 4	2 16	8 43
27	Sat	6 48	4 46	12 21	18	☌ ♂ ♄.J.H.Whe'ler d.'94		8 18	3 17	9 34

Fourth Sunday. Day's length 9 hours 57 minutes.

28	C.	6 49	4 46	12 21	28	Irving d. 1859.		9 29	4 12	10 26
29	Mo	6 50	4 46	11 21	38	Savannah taken1778		10 40	5 3	11 20
30	Tue	6 51	4 46	11 21	48	Fire at Durham 1880		11 47	5 49	0 1

RAILROAD BRAKE PATENTS.

Three thousand patents for railroad brakes alone have been issued by the Government; 7,000 for railway draft appliances, and 8,500 patents are classed under the head of railways. Four-fifths of these patents have been issued since 1880. During the year 1894, 684 patents were issued for improvements on cars and parts of cars, car-couplers alone receiving 218 patents.

STEAMSHIP RECORD.

The American Line steamer, "St. Louis," which arrived in New York on the afternoon of August 7th, 1896, broke the Southampton-New York record, making the passage in six days, two hours and 24 minutes, thus eclipsing the brilliant record made by her sister ship, the "St. Paul," the preceding June, of six days, five hours and 32 minutes.

GOVERNORS OF NORTH CAROLINA.

(Elected by the General Assembly.)

Elected.	Name.	County.	Died.
1776	Richard Caswell	Lenoir	1789
1779	Abner Nash	Craven	1789
1781	Thomas Burke	Orange	1783
1782	Alexander Martin	Guilford	1807
1784	Richard Caswell	Lenoir	1789
1787	Samuel Johnston	Chowan	1816
1789	Alexander Martin	Guilford	1807
1792	Richard Dobbs Speight, Sr	Craven	1802
1795	Samuel Ashe	New Hanover	1813
1798	Wm. R. Davie	Halifax	1820
1799	Benjamin Williams	Moore	1814
1802	John B. Ashe	Halifax	1802
1802	James Turner	Warren	1824
1805	Nathaniel Alexander	Mecklenburg	1808
1807	Benjamin Williams	Moore	1814
1808	David Stone	Bertie	1818
1810	Benjamin Smith	Brunswick	1829
1811	William Hawkins	Warren	1819
1814	William Miller	Warren	1826
1817	John Branch	Halifax	1863
1820	Jesse Franklin	Surry	1824
1821	Gabriel Holmes	Sampson	1829
1824	Hutchins G. Burton	Halifax	1836
1827	James Iredell	Chowan	1853

12th Month. DECEMBER, 1897. 31 Days.

Moon's Phases.

	D. H. M.		D. H. M.
🌕 Full Moon,	8 11 26p.m.	🌑 New Moon,	23 2 47p.m
☾ Last Quarter,	16 11 13p.m.	☽ First Quarter,	30 2 18p.m

Day of Month.	Day of Week.	Sun rises.	Sun sets.	Sun fast.	Sun's decline south.	ASPECTS OF PLANETS AND OTHER MISCELLANEOUS MATTER.	Moon's place.	Moon rises or sets.	Moon south.	High Tides.
1	We	6 51	4 46	11	21 57	Bat. of Austerlitz 1805.	♒	m'rn	eve.	m'rn
2	Thu	6 52	4 46	10	22 6	John Brown hung 1859.	♒	0 45	7 15	2 0
3	Fri	6 53	4 46	10	22 14	Bat. Hohenlinden 1800.	♓	1 46	7 57	3 0
4	Sat	6 54	4 46	9	22 22	Alabama admit. 1818.	♓	2 48	8 41	3 55
First Sunday.						Day's length 9 hours 51 minutes.				
5	C.	6 55	4 46	9	22 30		♈	3 49	9 25	4 45
6	Mo	6 56	4 46	9	22 37	Bedford Brown d. 1870.	♈	4 48	10 12	5 30
7	Tue	6 56	4 46	8	22 43	🌕 Ed. Badger d. 1878.	♉	5 46	11 1	6 13
8	We	6 67	4 46	8	22 49	☿ gr. Hel. Lat. S.	♉	6 41	11 51	6 52
9	Thu	6 58	4 46	7	22 55	☌ ♆ ☽. Milton b. 1608.	♉	rises.	m'rn	7 30
10	Fri	6 59	4 46	7	23 0	Dumas d. 1870.	♊	5 53	0 41	8 7
11	Sat	7 0	4 46	6	23 5	Indiana admitted 1816.	♊	6 51	1 31	8 44
Second Sunday.						Day's length 9 hours 46 minutes.				
12	C.	7 1	4 47	6	23 10	☌ ♆ ☉. Browning d. 1889	♋	7 50	2 20	9 20
13	Mo	7 2	4 47	5	23 13	Robt. Tombs d. 1884.	♋	8 51	3 7	9 58
14	Tue	7 3	4 47	5	23 17	HALCYON DAYS.	♋	9 53	3 52	10 39
15	We	7 3	4 47	4	23 20	☾ Sitting Bull k. 1890.	♌	10 58	4 36	11 25
16	Thu	7 4	4 48	4	23 22	Bost. Tea Barty 1773	♌	11 59	5 20	0 3
17	Fri	7 4	4 48	3	23 24	Poet Whitier b. 1807.	♍	m'rn	6 4	1 3
18	Sat	7 5	4 49	3	23 26	Humphrey Davy b. 1779	♍	0 5	6 52	2 5
Third Sunday.						Day's length 9 hours 43 minutes.				
19	C.	7 6	4 49	2	23 27	Gov. Holden imp. 1870.	♍	2 17	7 43	3 7
20	Mo	7 7	4 49	2	23 28	Washingt'n Duke b. 1820	♎	3 30	8 38	4 6
21	Tue	7 7	4 50	1	23 28	☉ ent. ♑. WINTER BEG.	♎	4 49	9 40	5 2
22	We	7 8	4 50		23 28	🌑 ☌ ♂ ☽.	♏	6 2	10 45	5 57
23	Thu	7 8	4 51	slow	23 27	H. W. Grady d. 1889.	♏	7 11	11 52	6 49
24	Fri	7 9	4 51		23 26	☌ ☿ ☽. Thackary d. 1863	♐	sets.	ev 56	7 40
25	Sat	7 9	4 52	1	23 24	CHRISTMAS DAY.	♐	7 5	1 56	8 29
Fourth Sunday.						Day's length 9 hours 44 minutes.				
26	C.	7 9	4 53	1	23 22	Girard d. 1831.	♑	8 18	2 51	9 18
27	Mo	7 10	4 53	2	23 19	☿ in ♌. St. John Evan.	♑	9 30	3 41	10 8
28	Tue	7 10	4 54	2	23 16	☿ stationery.	♒	10 37	4 27	10 58
29	We	7 10	4 54	2	23 12	W. E. Gladstone b. 1809.	♒	11 35	5 11	11 49
30	Thu	7 11	4 55	3	23 8	☽ ☌ ♀ ♂.	♓	m'rn	5 55	0 27
31	Fri	7 11	4 56	3	23 4	Bat. Murfreesb'ro '62	♓	0 40	6 38	1 25

DURHAM ALMANAC. 27

Elected.	Name.	County.	Died.
1828	John Owen	Bladen	1841
1830	Montford Stokes	Wilkes	1842
1832	David L. Swain	Buncombe	1868
1835	Richard Dobbs Speight, Jr	Craven	1850

ELECTED BY THE PEOPLE.

Elected.	Name.	County.	Died.
1837	Edward B. Dudley	New Hanover	1855
1841	John M. Morehead	Guilford	1866
1845	William A. Graham	Orange	1875
1849	Charles Manly	Wake	1871
1851	David S. Reid	Rockingham	1891
1854	Warren Winslow (ex-officio)	Cumberland	1862
1855	Thomas Bragg	Northampton	1872
1859	John W. Ellis	Rowan	1861
1861	Henry T. Clark (ex-officio)	Edgecombe	1874
1862	Zeb. B. Vance	Buncombe	1894
1865	W. W. Holden (Provisional)	Wake	1892
1865	Jonathan Worth	Randolph	1869
1868	W. W. Holden	Wake	1892
1870	Tod R. Caldwell	Burke	1874
1874	Curtis H. Brogden (ex-officio)	Wayne	
1877	Zeb. B. Vance	Buncombe	1894
1879	T. J. Jarvis	Pitt	
1885	Alfred M. Scales	Rockingham	1892
1889	Daniel G. Fowle	Wake	1891
1891	Thomas M. Holt (ex-officio)	Alamance	1896
1893	Elias Carr	Edgecombe	
1897	Daniel L. Russell	New Hanover	

NOTE.—In two instances father and son have been Governors, to-wit: R. D. Speight, Sr., in 1792, and R. D. Speight, Jr., in 1835; and Samuel Ashe in 1795, and John B. Ashe in 1802, he being elected that year, but died before inauguration. The elder Speight was killed in a duel by John Stanly at Newbern, 5th September, 1802.

GOVERNOR'S SALARIES.

New Jersey, New York, Pennsylvania	$10,000
Massachusetts and Ohio	8,000
California and Illinois	6,000
Colorado, Indiana, Kentucky, Minnesota, Missouri, Montana, Nevada, Virginia and Wisconsin	5,000
Maryland	4,500
Connecticut, Louisiana, Michigan, Mississippi, Tennessee, Texas and Washington	4,000
Iowa	3,600
Arizona, Arkansas, Florida, South Carolina and Utah	3,500
Alabama, Alaska, Georgia, Idaho, Kansas, North Carolina, North Dakota, Rhode Island	3,000
West Virginia	2,700

New Mexico and Oklahoma _____ 2,600
Nebraska, South Dakota and Wyoming_____ 2,500
Delaware, Maine and New Hampshire_____ 2,000
Oregon and Vermont_____ 1,500

☞ In thirty States the Governors receive higher salaries than does the Governor of North Carolina, varying from $3,500 to $10,000. Why not put the *Tar Heel* Governor at $7,500?

UNITED STATES SENATORS FROM NORTH CAROLINA.

Samuel Johnston—1789 to 1793. Chowan County. Born in Scotland, 1733; died near Edenton, 18th August, 1813.

Benjamin Hawkins—1789 to 1795. Warren County. Born 15th August, 1754; died 6th June, 1816.

Alexander Martin—1793 to 1799. Guilford County. Born in New Jersey, 1740. Graduate Princeton, 1756; died 1807 at Danbury.

Timothy Bloodworth—1795 to 1801. New Hanover County. Born 1736; died in Washington. N. C., 24th August, 1814. It is said of him, that he was by turns, "farmer, blacksmith, preacher, physician, wheelright and politician."

Jesse Franklin—1799 to 1805, 1807 to 1813. Surry County. Born 1758; died in Surry County, September, 1823. He was President *pro tem.* of Senate in 1804 and 1805.

David Stone—1801 to 1807, 1813 to 1814. Bertie County. Born at Hope, N. C., 17th February, 1770. Graduated at Princeton 1788. Died at Hope 7th October, 1818. He was censured by the Legislature for his opposition to President Madison's war measures, and he resigned his seat in 1814.

James Turner—1805 to 1816. Warren County. Born in Virginia, 1766; died at Bloomsbury, N. C., 15th January, 1824. He resigned in 1816, on account of ill health.

Francis Locke—1814 to 1815. Rowan County. Born 31st of October, 1766; died 8th January, 1823. He never took his seat and resigned in 1815.

Nathaniel Macon—1815 to 1828. Warren County. Born 1757; died suddenly in Warren County, 29th June, 1837. He was President *pro tem.* of the Senate, 19th and 20th Congresses—1826, 1828.

DURHAM ALMANAC. 29

Montford Stokes—1816 to 1823. Wilkes County. Born 1760; died in Arkansas Territory in 1842 (Indian Agent.)

John Branch—1823 to 1829. Halifax County. Born 4th November, 1782. Graduate U. N. C., 1801; died at Enfield, N. C., 4th January, 1863. He was re-elected in 1829, but resigned on 9th March to accept portfolio of the Navy under President Jackson, which he resigned in 1831.

James Iredell—1828 to 1831. Chowan County. Born 1788. Graduate Princeton 1806; died at Edenton, 13th April 1853.

Bedford Brown—1829 to 1840. Caswell County. Born 1795; died in Caswell County, 6th December, 1870. He resigned, because he would not obey instructions of the General Assembly.

Willie P. Mangum—1831 to 1836, 1841 to 1847, 1848 to 1853. Orange County. Born 29th December, 1792. Graduate University of N. C., 1815; died in Orange County 14th September, 1861. He resigned in 1836, declining to be instructed by the Legislature. He was President *pro tem.* of the Senate, 27th and 29th Congresses—1842 and 1846.

Robert Strange—1836 to 1840. Cumberland County. Born in Virginia 20th September, 1796; died in Fayetteville 10th February, 1854. He was elected to succeed W. P. Mangum, and he in turn also resigned, in 1840, declining to be instructed by the Legislature.

Wm. A. Graham—1840 to 1843. Orange County. Born 3d September, 1804; died at Saratoga Springs, 11th August, 1875. He was Confederate Senator from 22d February, 1864, to close of war, and Secretary of the Navy under President Fillmore.

Wm. H. Haywood—1843 to 1846. Wake County. Born 1801. Graduate University of North Carolina 1819; died in Raleigh 6th October, 1852. He resigned 25th July, 1846.

George E. Badger—1846 to 1855. Craven County. Born 13th April, 1795. Graduated at Yale 1813. Died in Raleigh 11th May, 1866. Was Secretary of Navy under President Harrison, and nominated as Justice Supreme Court by President Fillmore, but Senate refused to confirm him.

Asa Biggs—1853 to 1858. Martin County. Born 4th February, 1811; died in Norfolk, 6th March, 1878. He was appointed U. S. Judge under President Buchanan, and resigned his seat in the Senate in May, 1858.

David S. Reid—1854 to 1859. Rockingham County. Born 19th April, 1813; died 19th June, 1891.

Thomas Bragg—1859 to 1861. Warren County. Born 9th November, 1810; died in Raleigh 21st January, 1872. He resigned his seat early in 1861, and was elected Attorney General of the Confederates States 22d February, 1861.

Thos. L. Clingman—1858 to 1861. Buncombe County. Born 1811. Graduated at University of North Carolina 1832. He was appointed to fill vacancy of Asa Biggs, and elected for six years from 4th March, 1861, but he withdrew from the Senate 21st January, 1861, and was a Brigadier General in the Confederate States Army.

John Pool—1868 to 1873. Pasquotank County. Born 16th June, 1826; died in Washington City 18th August, 1884. Graduated at University North Carolina 1847. He was elected to the Senate in 1865, and re-elected in 1868. Took his seat in July, 1868.

Joseph C. Abbott—1868 to 1871. New Hanover County. Born in New Hampshire 15th July, 1825; died in Wilmington, 8th October, 1882. He was a Colonel in the United States army, and our only "carpet-bag" Senator.

A. S. Merrimon—1873 to 1879. Buncombe County. Born 15th September, 1830; died in Raleigh 14th November, 1892. At the time of his death he was Chief Justice Supreme Court of North Carolina.

M. W. Ransom—1872 to 1895. Northampton County. Born 8th October, 1826. Graduated at University of North Carolina 1847. His term of service was longer than any other Senator from the State. He is now U. S. Minister to Mexico.

Zebulon B. Vance—1878 to 1894. Buncombe County. Born 13th May, 1830; died in Washington City 15th April, 1894. No man ever lived in this State who was more loved in life and mourned in death, than our own "Zeb." Vance.

Thos. J. Jarvis—1894 to 1895. Pitt County. Born 18th January, 1836. Appointed by Gov. Carr to fill vacancy created by death of Senator Vance.

Marion Butler—1895. Sampson County. Born May 20th, 1863. Graduated at University of North Carolina 1885. Term expires 4th March, 1901.

J. C. Pritchard—1895 Madison County. Born 12th July, 1857. Term expires 4th March, 1897.

UNIVERSITY OF NORTH CAROLINA.

The Constitution of the State adopted at Halifax on the 18th of December, 1776, declared that a school or schools shall be established, and "all useful learning shall be duly encouraged and promoted in one or more Universities."

In accordance with the above, on the 7th of March, 1789, the "University of North Carolina" was established, by incorporating a Board of Trustees, naming Governor Samuel Johnston and others as said Board.

In November, 1792, the Trustees located the institution at Chapel Hill, the citizens of the neighborhood conveying to them 1180 acres of land.

In October, 1793, the first lots of the village were sold, and the corner-stone of the old East Building was laid (Oct. 12), with masonic honors, by Wm. R. Davie, Grand Master.

Rev. Dr. McCorkle one of the Trustees, delivered the address.

In 1795 the Trustees selected Rev. David Kerr as Professor, who was the University's first President, and Samuel A. Holmes, as Tutor.

The first student invading the classic shades of Chapel Hill, was Hinton James, of Wilmington, on the 12th of February, 1795.

President Kerr remained but a short time at the University, going from there (1796) to Lumberton, and afterwards to Mississippi, where he became a Judge, and died there in 1810. He was succeeded in the Presidency by Charles W. Harris, of Cabarrus County. He remained only one year, and was succeeded (1796) by Joseph Caldwell, a native of New Jersey and graduate of Princeton, 1791. He was appointed Professor of Mathematics in the fall of 1796, and in 1806 was made President of the University. In 1812 he resigned, and aided in procuring as his successor Rev. Robt. H. Chapman, D. D.—a New Jersey man, and graduate of Princeton in 1789. Dr. Chapman resigned in 1816, and Mr. Caldwell was again called to the chair, and he continued to hold the office till the day of his death, on the 27th of January, 1835, and he now sleeps beneath the royal shades of the beautiful college campus.

Dr. Caldwell was succeeded by Governor David L. Swain— known, respected, honored and loved by everybody as "Old

Bunk." He was elected to the Presidency in 1835, and well did he fill the illustrious Caldwell's place, until the doors of the University were closed in 1868, when all the Professors were summarily dismissed. Shortly after this (27th of August), Governor Swain died. In a few months the new Board of Trustees, (1868) elected a new President and faculty, who failed to command the confidence and support of the people of the State. It was maintained by an appropriation, and, after eighteen months' trial, and failure on their part, the Legislature of the State, (1870), solemnly ordered the institution to be closed.

Through the Alumni, the University was re-organized in 1875, and in the following year, 1876, Hon. Kemp P. Battle was elected President. The University moved forward with renewed vigor, and grew and prospered as it had never done before.

Dr. Battle resigned the presidency, preferring to take the chair of History, and George T. Winston was elected President, June, 1891. He resigned in the summer of 1896, having accepted the Presidency of the University of Texas. A called meeting of the Board of Trustees, was held in Raleigh on the 13th of August, 1896, for the purpose of electing a President. Many applications were filed by distinguished teachers, from this and other States. A goodly number of the Trustees were in attendance, and after mature deliberation and due consideration of the qualifications and merits of all the applicants, they *unanimously* conferred the honor upon Edwin A. Alderman, a native of New Hanover county and a graduate of the University in 1882. Surely they have made no mistake. As long as the Constitution of the State stands as it is, it is the duty of every good law abiding citizen to stand by the University.

"A State University is an institution of very great importance. It is a part of the government, is under its special protection and shares its dignity; and to allow it to be degraded, is to degrade ourselves. Without higher education no State can be great."—[MRS. C. P. SPENCER]

Take the SOUTHERN RAILWAY, passing through the cities of Alexandria, Charlottesville, Lynchburg, Danville, Greensboro, Reidsville, Salisbury, Columbia and Augusta, to the South and Southwest. For information, address W. A. Turk, G. P. A., Washington, D. C.

DURHAM ALMANAC.   33

UNIVERSITY APPROPRIATIONS.

The following amounts appropriated by the Legislatures of the various States, for the maintainance of their Universities, are taken from the Report of the Commissioner of the National Bureau of Education, page 123, for 1893-4, and are presumed to be authentic:

Wisconsin	$276,095	Texas	$ 46,200
Michigan	250,000	Indiana	44,000
Ohio	153,850	Virginia	40,000
New York	151,000	South Carolina	38,190
Illinois	141,882	Utah	37,500
California	120,137	North Dakota	36,900
Nebraska	118,170	Oregon	30,000
Kansas	85,000	South Dakota	28,550
Pennsylvania	72,500	West Virginia	25,700
Colorado	70,000	Nevada	25,000
Minnesota	69,500	Idaho	24,412
Iowa	67,000	North Carolina	20,000

GEORGIA'S EDUCATIONAL FACILITIES.

Georgia has, besides its flourishing State College, a Normal College, a College for Women, on the same basis as the Winthrop College in South Carolina, a great School of Technology at Atlanta, and four Agricultural Colleges—one for each section of the State. She is pushing the campaign of education right along. The Legislature has appropriated one million dollars for her schools.

OUT IN ILLINOIS.

At the last session of the Illinois Legislature an appropriation was made for the erection and equipment of an observatory. This makes four universities which have established Observatories in the past year, to-wit: Pennsylvania, at Philadelphia; Ohio, at Columbus; Minnesota, at Minneapolis; Illinois, at Champaign.

3

Hon. Richmond Pearson, in a recent letter to the *Charlotte Observer*, says:

"I shall be obliged if you will write me down as a friend of our State University. I have never seen the dear old place nor heard the sound of its bells—those bells were not tolling when I arrived at the collegiate age—and I missed advantages and associations, the thought of which makes me carry through life a nameless, pathetic regret. Though not one of her children, I know what this venerable institution has done for my State, and for the men who have gone before me, and I make bold to express the hope and belief that the Republican party, now restored to power, will not lay the hand of demolition upon the University, nor upon any other of our great institutions.

REMARKABLE RELIGIOUS STATISTICS.

There are, in North Carolina, 3,815 preachers, 7,378 churches, and 802,907 church members. The whites have 2,552 preachers, 5,094 churches, and 526,117 members. The colored have 1,263 preachers, 2,224 churches, and 276,799 members.

Among the whites, the Missionary Baptists take the lead, with 794 preachers, 1,577 churches, and 155,032 members, or, one preacher for every 195 members.

The Methodist Episcopal Church, South, comes next, with 661 preachers, 1,520 churches, and 128,691 members, or, one preacher for every 195 members.

The Presbyterians have 149 preachers, 366 churches, and 30,278 members, or, one preacher for every 203 members.

The Episcopalians have 96 preachers, 184 churches, and 9,025 members, or. one preacher for every 94 members.

The Primitive Baptists have 150 preachers, 317 churches, and 11,914 members, or, one preacher for every 79 members.

The Christians have 60 preachers, 103 churches, and 9,400 members, or, one preacher for every 157 members.

The Protestant Methodists have 64 preachers, 208 churches, and 16,416 members, or, one preacher for every 246 members.

The Quakers have 52 preachers, 52 churches, and 5,328 members, or one preacher for every 102 members.

DURHAM ALMANAC. 35

The Catholics have 24 preachers, 24 churches, and 2,640 members, or, one preacher for every 110 members.

Among the colored there is one preacher to every 219 members.

Taking all together, white and colored of all denominations, there is one preacher to every 210 members. About *one-half* the entire population are professing Christians. No wonder North Carolina is the *best* State in the American Union.

DURHAM CHURCH MEMBERSHIP.

Among the whites, the Methodists take the lead with 1,397 members; the Missionary Baptists have 1,017; the Presbyterians, 317; the Episcopalians, 166; the Christians, 85; the Primitive Baptists, 50, and the Catholic, 32. Making a total of 3,064. Among the colored the Missionary Baptists lead off with 990 members; the Methodists have 383; the Primitive Baptists, 67, and the Presbyterians 60. Making a total of 1,507, and grand total of white and colored of 4,507 members. Besides, there are in the town 142 Jews, and these wonderful people never settle in a dead town. Many of them here own valuable real estate.

VITALITY OF SEEDS.

Safe for two years.—Beans and Peas of all kinds, Peppers, Carrot, Egg Plant, Okra, Salsify, Thyme, Sage and Rhubarb.

Safe for three years.—Asparagus, Endive, Lettuce, Parsley, Spinach and Radish.

Safe for four years.—Broccoli, Cauliflower, Cabbage, Celery and Turnip.

Seeds possessing the greatest vitality are: Beet, Cucumber, Melon, Pumpkin, Squash and Tomato. These are good for from five to ten years.

WHAT TO PLANT AND WHEN.

From middle of February to end of March.—Beet, Cabbage, Carrot, Cauliflower, Celery, Cress, Endive, Kale, Lettuce, Onion, Parsley, Parsnip, Peas, Radish, Spinach, Turnip.

From first of April to middle of May.—Lima Beans, Bush Beans, Pole Beans, Tomato, Okra, Cucumber, Watermelon, Squash, Pumpkin, Nastrutium, Sweet Corn, Muskmelon.

MAN SUBJECT TO THE LAW OF NUMBERS AND PROPORTIONS.

The head is divided into four equal parts; from the top of the head to the forehead is the first; the forehead, to the top of the nose, is the second; the nose itself the third; and thence to the chin is the fourth.

The height of the figure is eight times the head, and divisible regularly into eight equal parts; and the arms, extended at full length, give the height of the body. Twice the circumference of the thumb is equal to the wrist; twice the wrist equals the neck, and twice the neck gives the circumference of the waist. Similar relations are found to exist throughout various parts of the body.

SOME TALL PEOPLE.

Charlemagne was seven feet. The Roman Emperor Maximus exceeded eight feet; Gabarus, in the reign of Claudius, was nine feet nine inches. The Emperor Andronicus was ten feet, and Pusio and Secondilla, in the reign of Augustus, are said to have been ten feet three inches in height.

CHINESE ECCENTRICITIES.

They read and write from right to left, and from foot of page to top

The surname precedes the given name.

They shake their own hands instead of shaking their friends' hands.

White is mourning with them, and dark colors are used on festive days.

They serve fruits and sweets first at dinner.

Their men are the only dressmakers.

Their compass points south instead of north.

They grieve at the birth of a child, and rejoice at its death.

They chop off the heads of defaulting cashiers.

DURHAM ALMANAC. 37

GOVERNMENT OF NORTH CAROLINA—1897-1901.

EXECUTIVE DEPARTMENT.

Daniel L. Russell, of New Hanover County, Governor; salary $3,000, and furnished house, fuel and lights.

James A. Reynolds, of Forsyth County, Lieutenant Governor and Speaker of the Senate.

Cyrus Thompson, of Onslow County, Secretary of State; salary $2,000 and fees; $1,000 additional assistance.

Hal W. Ayer, of Wake County, Auditor; salary $1,500; $1,000 additional for clerical assistance.

William H. Worth, of Wake County, Treasurer; salary $3,000.

Charles H. Mebane, of Catawba County, Superintendent of Public Instruction; salary $1,500; $500 per annum additional traveling expenses.

Zeb. Vance Walser, of Davidson Co., Attorney General; salary $2,000.

R. T. Gray, Reporter to Supreme Court; salary $750.

Francis H. Cameron, of Wake County, Adjutant General; salary $600.

J. C. Ellington, of Johnston County, State Librarian; salary $1,000.

C. M. Roberts, of Vance County, Superintendent of Public Buildings and Grounds; salary $850.

J. C. S. Lumsden, State Standard Keeper; salary $100.

University of North Carolina.

(Located in Chapel Hill, Orange County, twenty-eight miles northwest of Raleigh.)

Chartered in 1789, founded 1793, opened 1795. It now has in all departments 539 students and 35 instructors. The equipment includes twelve large buildings, five scientific laboratories, library of 40,000 volumes, campus of fifty acres with ample athletic grounds, gymnasium, &c. Perfect sanitation, baths, closets, &c. Tuition $60 a year, total expenses $200 to $300. Scholarships and loans for the needy. Law school and medical school. A summer school for teachers is conducted each July. It enrolled 153 teachers in 1896. The Faculty enrolled 19 Professors. During 1895 and 1896 many students supported themselves by labor, the total amount earned being about $5,000. The University is non-political and non-sectarian.

FACULTY.—Edwin Anderson Alderman, D. C. L., President and Professor of Political and Social Science ; Kemp Plummer Battle, LL. D., Professor of History ; Francis Preston Venable, Ph. D., Professor of General and Analytical Chemistry ; Joseph Austin Holmes, B. S., State Geologist and Lecturer on Geology of North Carolina ; Joshua Walker Gore, C. E., Professor of Natural Philosophy ; John Manning, LL. D., Professor of Law; Thomas Hume, D. D., LL. D., Professor of the English Languages and Literature ; Walter Dallam Toy, M. A., Professor of Modern Languages ; Eben Alexander, Ph. D., LL. D., Professor of the Greek Language and Literature (on leave of absence); William Cain, C. E., Professor of Mathematics ; Richard Henry Whitehead, M. D., Professor of Anatomy and Pathology ; Henry Horace Williams, A. M., B. D., Professor of Mental and Moral Science ; Henry Van Peters Wilson, Ph. D., Professor of Biology ; Karl Pomeroy Harrington, A. M., Professor of the Latin Languages and Literature ; James Shepherd, LL. D., Ex-Chief Justice of the Supreme Court of North Carolina, and Associate Professor of Common and Statute Law and Equity in Summer School ; Collier Cobb, A. M., Professor of Geology ; Francis Kingsley Ball, Ph. D., Professor of Greek ; Charles Baskerville, Ph. D., Assistant Professor of

Chemistry ; Charles Staples Mangum, A. B., Professor of Physiology and Materia Medica ; —— ——, Professor of Pedagogy ; George Phineas Butler, B. E., Instructor in Mathematics ; Samuel May, A. B., Instructor in Modern Languages ; Henry Farrar Linscott, A. B., Instructor in Latin ; William Robert Webb, Jr., A. B., Instructor in English; William Cunningham Smith, Ph. B., Instructor in Pedagogies ; Harry Ellsworth Mechling, Director of Gymnasium ; Robert Ervin Coke, S B., Assistant in Biology ; George Hughes Kirby, S B., Assistant in Biology ; Arthur Williams Belden, Assistant in Chemistry ; John Gilchrist McCormick, Assistant in Geology ; Arch Turner Allen, Assistant in Physics ; Stanford Hunter Harris, Assistant in Chemistry ; Collier Cobb, A. M., Secretary of Faculty ; Francis Kingsley Ball, Ph. D., Supervisor of Library ; Benjamin Wyche, Litt. B., Librarian; Eugene Lewis Harris, Ph. B., Registrar; Willie Thomas Patterson, Bursar.

PUBLIC WORKS AND INSTITUTIONS IN NORTH CAROLINA.

North Carolina Department of Agriculture.

Located at Raleigh, in a building especially arranged for the purpose, immediately north of Capitol Square.

OFFICERS.—S. L. Patterson, Commissioner ; T. K. Bruner, Secretary ; H. B. Battle, Ph. D., Chemist and Director Experiment Station.

N. C. Agricultural Experiment Station, including the Fertilizer Control Station and State Weather Service, Raleigh, N. C.

The officers of the Station are : H. B. Battle, Ph. D., Director and State Chemist; F. E. Emery, B. S., Agriculturist ; Gerald McCarthy, B. Sc., Botanist and Entomologist ; W. F. Massey, C. E., Horticulturist; C. F. von Herrmann, U. S. Weather Bureau, Meteorologist; F. P. Williamson, D. V. S., Consulting Veterinarian ; B. W. Kilgore, M. S., Assistant Chemist; F. B. Carpenter, B. S., Assistant Chemist ; W. M. Allen, Assistant Chemist; C. B. Williams, B. S., Assistant Chemist; Roscoe Nunn, U. S. Weather Bureau, Assistant Meteorologist ; Alex. Rhodes, Assistant Horticulturist ; A F. Bowen, Secretary.

N. C. College of Agriculture and Mechanic Arts.

FACULTY AND OFFICERS.—Alexander Q. Holladay, President ; W. F. Massey, C. E., Professor of Horticulture, Arboriculture and Botany ; W. A. Withers, A. M , Professor of Pure and Agricultural Chemistry; D. H. Hill, A. M., Professor of English ; B. Irby, M. S., Professor of Agriculture ; W. C. Riddick, A. B., C. E., Professor of Mechanics and Applied Mathematics ; Lieut. Richard Henderson, U. S. N., Professor of Military Tactics and Physics ; R. E. L. Yates, A. M., Adjunct Professor of Mathematics ; F. E. Emery, B. S., Assistant Professor of Agriculture ; Charles M. Pritchett, B S., Instructor in Mechanics ; Charles B. Park, Instructor in Practical Mechanics ; L. T. Yarborough and C. E. Pearson, Assistant in Shops ; S. E. Asbury, B. S., Instructor in Chemistry ; B. S. Skinner, Assistant in Agricultural and Horticultural Practice ; B. F. Walton, B S., Assistant in Dairy ; Professor Withers, Secretary of the Faculty ; Professor Hill, Bursar ; Mr. Skinner, Superintendent of the Farm ; Mrs. Sue C. Carroll, Matron ; J. R. Rogers, M. D., Physician.

Take the SOUTHERN RAILWAY, passing through the cities of Alexandria, Charlottesville, Lynchburg, Danville, Greensboro, Reidsville, Salisbury, Columbia and Augusta, to the South and Southwest. For information, address W. A. Turk, G. P. A.. Washington, D. C.

DURHAM ALMANAC.   39

North Carolina Agricultural Society.

OFFICERS.—Benehan Cameron, President, Durham; John Nichols, Secretary and Treasurer, Raleigh.

VICE PRESIDENTS.—(Permanent)—Hon. Kemp P. Battle, Orange; R. H. Battle, Wake.

Officers N. C. State Penitentiary.

A. Leazar, Superintendent; John M. Fleming, Warden: William Ledbetter, Deputy Warden; J. W. McGee, Physician; J. J. Bernard, Clerk.

North Carolina Institution for the Blind.

The North Carolina Institution for the Blind is located at Raleigh.

OFFICERS.—John E. Ray, Principal; Dr. Hubert Haywood. of Raleigh, Physician; W. H. Rand. Steward; W. H. Worth, ex officio Treasurer.

North Carolina School for the Deaf and Dumb.

Located at Morganton, N. C.

OFFICERS —E. McK. Goodwin, Superintendent; George L. Phifer, Steward; Mrs. Mary B. Malone, Matron; E. S. Walton, Deputy Treasurer.

North Carolina Insane Asylum.

Situated in the vicinity of Raleigh, and will accommodate four hundred patients.

OFFICERS —W. H. Worth, ex officio Treasurer; W. T. Smith, Esq., Keeper of Records.

RESIDENT OFFICERS.—Dr. George L Kirby, Superintendent; Dr. J. A. Faison, 1st Assistant Physician: Dr. R. S. McGeachey. 2d Assistant Physician; W. R. Crawford, Jr., Steward; Mrs. M. A. Whitaker, Matron.

The State Hospital, Morganton.

OFFICERS.—P. L. Murphy, M. D., Superintendent; Isaac M. Taylor, M. D., Assistant Physician; T. S. Mott, M. D., Assistant Physician; F. M. Scroggs, Steward; Mrs. C. A. Marsh, Matron.

Eastern Hospital, Goldsboro, for Colored People.

J. F. Miller, M. D., Superintendent; W. W. Faison, M. D., Assistant Physician; Daniel Reid, Steward; Mrs. B. V. Smith, Matron.

Bureau of Labor Statistics.

B. R. Lacy. Wake County, Commissioner; W. E. Faison,Wake County, Clerk. Office in the Supreme Court Building.

N. C. Board of Railroad Commissioners.

COMMISSIONERS.—J. W. Wilson, Burke County, Chairman; E. C. Beddingfield, Wake County; S. Otho Wilson, Wake County. H. C. Brown, Surry County, Clerk.

Regular sessions of the Court are held at Raleigh. Special sessions are also held at other places, under such regulations as are made by the Commissioners.

Offices of the Commissioners are located in the Agricultural Building.

North Carolina Geological Survey.

Jos. A. Holmes, State Geologist; H. B. C. Nitze, Assistant Geologist; J. V. Lewis, Assistant Geologist; W. W. Ashe, Forester

State Museum.

In the Agricultural Building at Raleigh, under the control of the Board of Agriculture. Jos. A. Holmes and T. K. Bruner, Directors; H. H. Brimley, Curator.

Medical Board of Examiners of North Carolina.

Dr. W. H. Whitehead, Rocky Mount, President; Dr. L. J. Picot, Littleton, Secretary; Dr. George W. Long, Graham; Dr. H. B. Weaver, Asheville; Dr. Julian M. Baker, Tarboro; Dr. J. M. Hays, Greensboro; Dr. Thomas S. Burbank, Wilmington.

North Carolina Board of Health.

George G. Thomas, M. D., Wilmington; S. Westray Battle, M. D., Asheville; W. H. Harrell, M. D., Williamston; W. P. Beall, M. D., Greensboro; W. J. Lumsden, M. D., Elizabeth City; John Whitehead, M. D., Salisbury; F. P. Venable, Ph. D., Chapel Hill; J. C. Chase, Civil Engineer, Wilmington; Richard H. Lewis, M. D., Raleigh, Secretary and Treasurer.

Board of Public Charities of North Carolina.

Chas. Duffy, M. D., Chairman, Craven County; Lawrence J. Haughton, Chatham County; Wesley N. Jones, Wake County; William A. Blair, Forsyth County; S. W. Reid, Mecklenburg County; C. B. Denson, Wake County, Secretary.

State Normal and Industrial School, Greensboro.

Charles D. McIver, A. B., Litt. D., President; Miss Sue May Kirkland, Lady Principal; E. J. Forney, Bursar; Annie M. Petty, Librarian; Mrs. W. P. Carraway, Matron.

Supreme Court of North Carolina.

William T. Faircloth, of Wayne, Chief Justice; Robert M. Douglass, of Guilford County; Walter Clark, of Wake County; David M. Furches, of Iredell County, and Walter A. Montgomery, of Wake County, Associate Justices. Salary $2,500 each.

Thos. S. Kenan, Clerk, salary $300 and fees.

Robert T. Gray, Reporter, salary $750.

Robert H. Bradley, Marshal and Librarian, salary $1,000.

J. L. Seawell, office Clerk.

The Court meets in Raleigh on the first Monday in February, and the last Monday in September of each year.

Spring Term—1st Judicial District, February 1st; 2d District, February 8th; 3d District, February 15th; 4th District, February 22d; 5th District, March 1st; 6th District, March 8th; 7th District, March 15th; 8th District, March 22d; 9th District, March 29th; 10th District, April 5th; 11th District, April 12th; 12th District, April 19th.

Fall Term—1st District, September 27th; 2d District October 4th; 3d District, October 11th; 4th District, October 18th; 5th District, October 25th; 6th District, November 1st; 7th District, November 8th; 8th District, November 15th; 9th District, November 22d; 10th District, November 29th; 11th District, December 6th; 12th District, December 13th.

Applicants for license to practice law are examined on Monday, the first day of each term.

United States Supreme Court.

Chief Justice, Melville W. Fuller, $10,500.

There are eight Associate Justices, who each receive $10,000 a year salary, as follows: Stephen Johnson Field, John Marshal Harlan, Horace Gray, David Josiah Brewer, Henry Billings Brown, George Shiras, Jr., Edward D. White, Rufus W. Peckham.

Take the SOUTHERN RAILWAY, passing through the cities of Alexandria, Charlottesville, Lynchburg, Danville, Greensboro, Reidsville, Salisbury, Columbia and Augusta, to the South and Southwest. For information, address W. A. Turk, G. P. A., Washington, D. C.

DURHAM ALMANAC. 41

SUPERIOR COURTS OF NORTH CAROLINA FOR 1897.

JUDGES.

Name.	District.	Residence.
George H. Brown,	1	Washington.
Henry R. Bryan,	2	Newbern.
E. W. Timberlake,	3	Louisburg.
W. S. O'B. Robinson,	4	Goldsboro.
Spencer B. Adams,	5	Yanceyville.
Oliver H. Allen,	6	Kinston.
James D. McIver,	7	Carthage.
Albert L. Coble,	8	Statesville.
Henry R. Starbuck,	9	Winston.
Leander L. Green,	10	Boone.
W. Alexander Hoke,	11	Lincolnton.
W. L. Norwood.	12	Waynesville.

SOLICITORS.

Name,	District.	Residence.
W. J. Leary,	1	Eliz'b'th City.
W. E. Daniel,	2	Weldon.
C. M. Bernard,	3	Greenville.
Edward W. Pou, Jr.,	4	Smithfield.
W. P. Bynum, Jr.,	5	Greensboro.
Milton C. Richardson,	6	Clinton.
H. F. Seawell,	7	Carthage.
J. Q. Holton,	8	Yadkinville.
M. L. Mott,	9	Wilkesboro.
J. F. Spainhour,	10	Lenoir.
J. L. Webb,	11	Shelby.
George A. Jones,	12	Franklin.

Time of Holding Courts.

FIRST JUDICIAL DISTRICT.

Spring—Judge Bryan.

Fall—Judge Brown.

Beaufort—‡Feb. 15th (2), May 24th (2), Nov. 29th (2).
Currituck—March 1st, Sept. 6th.
Camden—March 8th, Sept. 13th.
Pasquotank—March 15th, Sept. 20th.
Perquimans—March 22d, Sept. 27th.
Chowan—March 29th, October 4th.
Gates—April 5th, Oct. 11th.
Hertford—April 12th, Oct. 18th.
Washington—April 19th, June 7th, Oct. 25th.
Tyrrell—April 26th, Nov. 1st.
Dare—May 3d, Nov. 8th
Hyde—May 10th, Nov. 15th.
Pamlico—May 17th, Nov. 22d.

SECOND JUDICIAL DISTRICT.

Spring—Judge Timberlake.

Fall—Judge Bryan.

Halifax—March 1st (2), May 24th (2), Nov. 22d (2).
Northampton—March 29th (2), †Aug. 2d (2), Oct. 25th (2).
Bertie—‡Feb. 15th, April 26th, ‡Sept. 13th (2), Nov. 8th.
Craven—‡Feb. 1st (2), May 3d (2). Nov. 29th (2).
Warren—March 15th (2), Sept. 20th (2).
Edgecombe—April 12th (2), †June 14th (2), Oct. 11th (2).

THIRD JUDICIAL DISTRICT.

Spring—Judge Robinson.

Fall—Judge Timberlake.

Pitt—Jan. 4th (2), †March 1st (2), March 29th, (2), Sept. 27th (2), †Dec. 6th (2).
Franklin—Jan. 18th (2), April 12th (2), Oct. 25th.
Wilson—‡Feb. 1st (2), May 31st (2), Nov. 1st (2).
Vance—Feb. 15th (2), May 17th (2), Oct. 4th (2).
Martin—March 15th (2), Sept. 6th (2).
Nash—April 26th (2), Nov. 22d (2).

FOURTH JUDICIAL DISTRICT.

Spring—Judge Adams.

Fall—Judge Robinson.

Wake—*Jan. 4th (2), †Feb. 22d (2), *Mar. 22d (2), †April 19th (2), *July 12th (2), *Sept. 27th (2), †Oct. 25th (3).

Wayne—Jan. 18th (2), April 12th, Sept. 13th (2), Oct. 18th.
Harnett—Feb. 15th, Sept. 6th, ‡Nov. 29th.
Johnston—March 8th (2), Aug. 30th, Nov. 15th (2).

FIFTH JUDICIAL DISTRICT.

Spring—Judge Allen.

Fall—Judge Adams.

Durham—Jan. 11th (2), †March 22d (2), *May 10th, *Sept. 13th, †Oct. 11th (2).
Granville—Jan. 25th (2), April 19th (2), July 26th (2), Nov. 29 (2).
Chatham—Feb. 8th, May 3d. Sept. 27th (2).
Guilford—Feb. 15th (2), May 24th, Aug. 30th (2), Dec. 13th (2).
Alamance—March 8th, May 17th, Nov. 15th.
Orange—March 15th, Aug. 9th, Nov 1.
Caswell—April 5th, Aug. 16th, Oct. 25th.
Person—April 12th, Aug. 23d, Nov. 22d.

SIXTH JUDICIAL DISTRICT.

Spring—Judge McIver.

Fall—Judge Allen.

Pender—March 1st, Sept. 13th (2).
Greene—Feb. 22d, Aug. 16th, Nov. 29th.
New Hanover—†Jan. 18th (2), †April 12th (2), †Sept. 27th (2).
Lenoir—May 3d (2), Nov. 15th (2).
Duplin—Feb. 15th, Aug. 9th, Dec. 6th.
Sampson—Feb. 1st (2), April 26th, Oct. 11th (2).
Carteret—March 15th, Oct. 25th.
Jones—March 22d, Nov. 1st.
Onslow—March 29th, Nov. 8th.

SEVENTH JUDICIAL DISTRICT.

Spring—Judge Coble.

Fall—Judge McIver.

Columbus—†Feb. 22d, July 19th, Nov. 8th.
Anson—*Jan. 4th, †April 26th, *Sept. 6th, †Nov. 29th.
Cumberland—*Jan. 18th, †April 19th (2), †May 10th, *July 26th, †Nov. 15th (2).
Robeson—Jan. 25th (2), May 17th, †Aug. 2d (3), Oct. 4th (2).
Richmond—*Feb. 15th (2), †April 12th, May 31st, *†Sept. 20th, Nov. 1st. Dec. 6th.
Bladen—March 15th (2), Oct. 25th.
Brunswick—April 5th, *†Sept. 13th.
Moore—†Jan. 11th, March 1st (2), *†Aug. 16th (3), *Dec. 13th.

SUPERIOR COURTS—Continued.

EIGHTH JUDICIAL DISTRICT.

Spring—Judge Starbuck.

Fall—Judge Coble.

Cabarrus—Jan. 18th (2), July 26th (2).
Iredell—Feb. 1st (2), May 17th (2), Aug. 9th (2), Nov. 8th.
Rowan—Feb. 15th (2), May 10th, Aug. 23d (2), Nov 22d (2).
Davidson—March 1st (2), Sept. 6th (2).
Randolph—March 15th (2), July 12th (2), Nov. 15th.
Montgomery—March 29th, Oct. 4th (2).
Yadkin—May 3d, Oct. 25th (2).

NINTH JUDICIAL DISTRICT

Spring—Judge Green.

Fall—Judge Starbuck.

Alexander—Jan. 18th, July 19th.
Rockingham—Jan. 25th (2), July 26th, Nov. 1st (2).
Forsyth—Feb. 15th (2), May 10th (2), Aug. 9th (2), Dec. 6th (2).
Wilkes—March 1st (2), Sept. 6th (2).
Alleghany—March 29th, Sept. 20th.
Davie—April 5th (2), Sept. 27th (2).
Stokes—April 19th (2), Oct. 18th (2).
Surry—March 15th (2), Oct. 11th (2).

TENTH JUDICIAL DISTRICT.

Spring—Judge Hoke.

Fall—Judge Green.

Catawba—Feb. 15th (2), Aug. 2d (2).
McDowell—March 1st (2), Aug. 16th (2).
Burke—March 15th (2), Aug. 30th (2).
Caldwell—March 29th (2), Sept. 13th (2).
Ashe—April 12th, Sept. 27th (2).

Watauga—April 26th, Oct. 11th.
Mitchell—May 3d (2), Oct. 18th (2).
Yancey—May 17th, Nov. 1st (2).

ELEVENTH JUDICIAL DISTRICT.

Spring—Judge Norwood.

Fall—Judge Hoke.

Union—*†Jan. 25th *†Aug. 23d (2).
Stanly—March 1st (2), Sept. 6th (2).
Mecklenburg—†Jan. 18th, †March 15th (2), †May 31st, †Oct. 4th (2).
Gaston—†Feb. 15th, Sept. 20th (2).
Lincoln—March 29th (2), Oct. 18th.
Cleveland—April 12th (2), Oct. 25th (2).
Rutherford—April 26th (2), Nov. 8th (2).
Polk—May 10th, Nov. 22d.
Henderson—†May 17th (2),†Nov. 29th (2)

TWELFTH JUDICIAL DISTRICT.

Spring—Judge Brown.

Fall—Judge Norwood.

Madison—†Feb. 2d (2), †Aug. 2d (2).
Buncombe—†March 8th (3), †Aug. 16th (3), †Dec. 6th (2).
Transylvania—March 29th, Sept 6th.
Haywood—†April 5th (2), †Sept 13th (2).
Jackson—April 19th (2), Sept. 27th.
Macon—May 3d, Oct. 4th.
Clay—May 10th, Oct. 11th.
Cherokee—*†May 17th (2),*†Oct. 18th (2).
Graham—May 31st, Nov. 8th (2).
Swain—June 7th (2), Nov. 22d (2).

*For criminal cases.
†For civil cases alone.
‡For civil cases alone except jail cases.
(2)Means two weeks, etc.

NOTE.—The above is subject to any and all sorts of changes that the General Assembly may see fit to make.

CRIMINAL COURTS.

EASTERN DISTRICT.

Judge—Oliver P. Mears, Wilmington.
New Hanover—*Jan. 4th, March 8th, Oct. 11th.
Warren—Jan. 18th, July 12th.
Vance—Jan. 25th, Sept. 13th.
Edgecombe—Feb. 8th, Nov. 1st.
Craven—Feb. 15th, Oct. 4th.
Halifax—Feb. 22d, Dec. 6th.
Mecklenburg—April 12th, Sept. 6th.
Robeson—April 19th.

WESTERN DISTRICT.

Buncombe, Haywood, Madison and Henderson: Judge, Hamilton G. Ewart, Hendersonville ; Solicitor, Robert S. McCall, Asheville ; Clerk, W. H. Wilson.
Haywood—Jan. 11th, June 28th.
Buncombe—Jan. 25th, April 26th, July 26th, Oct. 25th.
Madison—Feb. 8th, June 4th, Nov. 8th.
Henderson—April 12th, Oct. 11th.

U. S. CIRCUIT AND DISTRICT COURTS.

Charles H Simonton, Charleston, S. C., Judge of Fourth Circuit of U. S. Courts.
Nathan Goff, West Virginia, Judge of U. S. Circuit Court of Appeals for Fourth District.
WESTERN DISTRICT.—R. P. Dick, Greensboro, Judge ; R. B. Glenn, District Attorney; D. A. Covington, Assistant Attorney ; S. L. Trogden, Clerk. *Greensboro*—Circuit and District—April 5th, October 4th. *Statesville*—Circuit and District—H. C. Cowles, Clerk; April 19th, October 18th. *Asheville*—Circuit and District—R. O. Patterson, Clerk ; May 3d, Nov 1st. *Charlotte*—Circuit and District—H. C. Cowles, Clerk ; June 7th, Dec. 13th. EASTERN DISTRICT—A. S. Seymour, Judge ; C. B. Aycock, Goldsboro, District Attorney ; Sol. C. Weil, Wilmington, Assistant Attorney ; W. C. Brooks, Clerk. *Elizabeth City*—District Court—April 19th, October 18th. *Newbern*—District Court—Geo. Green, Clerk ; April 26th, October 25th. *Wilmington*—Circuit and District—N. J. Riddick, Clerk ; V. Royster, Assistant Clerk in Raleigh ; W. H. Shaw, Clerk of District and Deputy of Circuit Court at Wilmington ; O. J. Carroll, Marshal; May 3d, November 1st. *Raleigh*—Circuit Court—N. J. Riddick, Clerk ; V. Royster, Assistant Clerk in Raleigh ; W. H. Shaw, Clerk of District and Deputy of Circuit Court at Wilmington ; O. J. Carroll, Marshal, May 24th, December 6th.

DURHAM ALMANAC. 43

N. C. Representatives in Congress.

Senate.—Jeter C. Pritchard; term expires 4th March, 1897. Marion Butler; term expires 4th March, 1901.

House of Representatives.—1st District, Harry Skinner. Populist; 2d District, George H. White, Rep.; 3d District, Jno. E. Fowler, Pop.; 4th District, W. F. Stroud. Pop.; 5th District, W. W. Kitchen, Dem.; 6th District, Chas. H. Martin, Pop.; 7th District, A. C. Shuford, Pop.; 8th District, R. Z. Linney, Rep.; 9th District, Richmond Pearson, Rep.

MEMBERS OF THE GENERAL ASSEMBLY OF NORTH CAROLINA FOR 1897-'98.

SENATE.

First District—Currituck, Camden, Pasquotank, Hertford, Gates, Chowan and Perquimans—two Senators: Jno. F. Newsome, Pop., Winton ; J. L. Whidbee, Rep., Hertford.

Second District—Tyrrell, Washington. Martin, Dare. Beaufort, Hyde and Pamlico—two Senators: T. E. McCaskey, Pop., Dardens ; N. B. Yeager, Rep., Plymouth.

Third District— Northampton and Bertie—one Senator: J. M. Early, Pop., Aulander.

Fourth District — Halifax—one Senator: E.T.Clark, Pop., Weldon.

Fifth District—Edgecombe—one Senator: Lee W. Person, Rep., Rocky Mount.

Sixth District—Pitt—one Senator: A. J. Moye, Pop.. Farmville.

Seventh District—Wilson, Nash and Franklin—two Senators: J. F. Mitchell, Pop., Franklinton; J. T. Sharp, Rep., Elm City.

Eighth District—Craven, Jones, Carteret, Lenoir, Greene and Onslow—two Senators: G. L. Hardison, Pop., Thurman; W. T. McCarthy, Rep., Newbern,

Ninth District—Duplin, Wayne and Pender—two Senators: R. G. Maxwell, Pop., Outlaw's Bridge ; H. L. Grant, Rep., Goldsboro

Tenth District—New Hanover and Brunswick—one Senator: Geo. H. Cannon, Pop., Town Creek.

Eleventh District — Warren and Vance—one Senator: W. B. Henderson, Rep., Henderson.

Twelfth District — Wake — one Senator: C. H. Utley, Pop., Holly Springs.

Thirteenth District—Johnston—one Senator: E. S. Abell, Dem., Smithfield.

Fourteenth District—Sampson, Harnett and Bladen—two Senators: Geo. E. Butler, Pop., Clinton; E. N. Roberson, Pop., Tar Heel.

Fifteenth District — Columbus and Robeson—two Senators: Angus Shaw, Pop., Maxton ; J. D. Maultsby, Rep., Whiteville.

Sixteenth District—Cumberland —one Senator: John McP. Geddy, Pop., Cedar Creek.

Seventeenth District —Granville and Person—one Senator: Dr. Wm. Merritt, Pop., Bethel Hill.

Eighteenth District—Caswell, Alamance, Orange and Durham—two Senators: J. E. Lyon, Pop., Durham; E. S. Parker, Dem., Graham.

Nineteenth District—Chatham—one Senator: John W. Atwater, Pop., Rialto.

Twentieth District — Rockingham—one Senator : J. A. Walker, Pop., Monroeton.

Twenty-first District—Guilford —one Senator: Alfred M. Scales, Dem., Greensboro.

Twenty-second District — Randolph and Moore—one Senator: D. Reid Parker, Pop., Trinity.

Twenty-third District — Richmond, Montgomery, Anson and Union—two Senators: W. H. Odom, Pop., Wadesboro; D. A. Patterson, Pop., Rockingham.

Twenty-fourth District—Cabarrus and Stanly—one Senator: C. D. Barringer, Dem., Mt. Pleasant.

Twenty-fifth District—Mecklenburg—one Senator Dr. J. B. Alexander, Pop., Charlotte.

Twenty-sixth District—Rowan, Davidson and Forsyth—two Senators: S. A. Earnhardt, Pop., Salisbury; Jno. A. Ramsey, Rep., Salisbury.

Twenty-seventh District — Iredell, Davie and Yadkin—two Senters: A. C. Sharpe, Rep., Fancy Hill; S. F. Shore, Rep., Shore.

Twenty-eighth District—Stokes and Surry—one Senator: Rev. Jesse A. Ashburn, Rep., Pilot Mountain.

Twenty-ninth District—Catawba, Lincoln, Wilkes and Alexander—two Senators: R. H. W. Barker, Pop., Harvey; Milton McNeill, Rep., Wilkesboro.

Thirtieth District — Alleghany, Ashe and Wautauga—one Senator: J. M. Dixon, Rep., Idol.

Thirty-first District — Caldwell, Burke, McDowell, Mitchell and Yancey — two Senators: E. F. Wakefield, Pop., Lenoir; James L. Hyatt, Rep., Mica.

Thirty-second District—Gaston, Cleveland, Rutherford and Polk—two Senators: J T. Anthony, Dem., Shelby; M. H. Justice, Dem., Rutherfordton.

Thirty-third District—Buncombe, Madison and Haywood—two Senators: W. W. Rollins, Rep., Asheville; George H. Smathers, Rep., Waynesville.

Thirty-fourth District—Henderson, Transylvania, Jackson and Swain—one Senator: H. S. Anderson, Rep., Hendersonville.

Thirty-fifth District — Macon, Cherokee, Clay and Graham—one Senator: Frank Ray, Dem., Franklin.

HOUSE.

Alamance—S. A. White, Rep. Mebane.

Alexander—J. W. Watts, Dem., Taylorsville.

Alleghany—H. F. Jones, Pop., Sparta.

Anson—James F. Leak, Dem., Wadesboro.

Ashe—Spencer Blackburn, Rep., Jefferson.

Beaufort—H. E. Hodges, Pop., Mineola.

Bertie—K. W. White, Rep., Windsor.

Bladen—Sidney Meares, Rep., Clarkton.

Brunswick—W. W. Drew, Pop., El Paso.

Buncombe—V. S. Lusk, Rep., Asheville; W. G. Candler, Pop., Candler.

Burke—Jno. H. Pearson, (Silver) Morganton.

Cabarrus—A. F. Hileman, Pop., Concord.

Caldwell—J. L. Nelson. Dem., Lenoir.

Camden—Jas. E. Burgess, Rep., Old Trap.

Curteret—E. C. Duncan, Rep., Beaufort.

Caswell—C. J. Yarborough, Pop., Locust Hill.

Catawba—L. R. Whitener, Pop., Hickory.

Chowan—Richard Elliott, Rep., Cisco.

Chatham—J. E. Bryan, Pop., Moncure; L. L. Wrenn, Rep., Siler City.

Cherokee—D. W. Deweese, Rep., Murphy.

Clay—W. F. Plott, Pop., Warner.

Cleveland—Dr. B. F. Dixon, Dem., Kings Mountain.

Columbus—J. B. Schulken, Pop., Whiteville.

Craven—Robt. Hancock, Rep., Newbern.

DURHAM ALMANAC. 45

Cumberland—Thos. H. Sutton, Rep., Fayetteville; W. P. Wemyss, Rep., Fayetteville.

Currituck—W. H. Gallop, Dem., Harbinger.

Dare—George C. Daniels, Rep., Wauchese.

Davidson—J. R. McCreary, Rep., Lexington.

Davie—W. A. Bailey, Rep., Advance.

Duplin—Maury Ward, Pop., Joford.

Durham—J. W. Umstead, Dem., Flat River.

Edgecombe—J. H. Dancy, Rep., Tarboro; E. Bryan, Rep., Tarboro.

Forsyth — J. L. Grubb, Rep., Walkertown; W. P. Ormsby, Rep., Salem.

Franklin—W. T. Barrow, Pop., Youngsville.

Gaston—S. M. Wilson, Dem., Gastonia.

Gates—T. H. Rountree, Pop., Druanan.

Graham—John Dayton, Rep., Robbinsville.

Granville—John King, Pop.; Buchanan; W. H. Crews, Rep., Oxford.

Greene—W. R. Dixon, Pop., Farmville.

Guilford—John T. Burch, Dem., Oak Ridge; B. G. Chilcutt, Rep., Brown's Summit.

Halifax—Scotland Harris, Rep., Littleton; J. H. Arrington, Rep., Halifax.

Harnett—L. B. Chapin, Rep., Summerville.

Haywood—Jas. Ferguson, Dem., Waynesville.

Henderson—J. B. Freeman, Rep., Fruitland.

Hertford—Starkey Hare, Rep., Tunis.

Hyde—John G. Harris, Pop., Fairfield.

Iredell—J. R. McLelland, Dem., Mooresville; J. A. Hartness, Dem., Statesville.

Jackson—J. B. Ensley, Rep., Beta.

Johnston—C. W. Smith, Dem., Princeton; C. M. Creech, Dem., Clayton.

Jones—H. F. Brown, Pop., Tuckahoe.

Lenoir—E. P. Hauser, Pop., Kinston.

Lincoln—L. A. Abernethy, Pop., Macpelah.

Macon—Dr. S. H. Lyle, Dem., Franklin.

Madison—J. W. Roberts, Rep., Marshall.

Martin—C. C. Fagan, Pop., Darden.

McDowell—W. A. Conley, Dem., Marion.

Mecklenburg — W. P. Craven, Pop., Bristow; J. Sol. Reid, Dem., Matthews; R. M. Ransom, Dem., Huntersville.

Mitchell—Rev. L. H. Green, Rep., Bakersville.

Montgomery—J. A. Reynolds, Pop., Okeweeme.

Moore—Rev. W. H. H. Lawhorn, Dem., Carthage.

Nash—Van B. Carter, Pop., Elm City.

New Hanover—D. B. Sutton, Rep., Wilmington; J. T. Howe, Rep., Wilmington.

Northampton—N. R. Rawls, Rep., Garysburg.

Onslow—R. Duffy, Dem., Catherine Lake.

Orange—A. R. Holmes, Pop., Rock Spring.

Pamlico—C. M. Babbitt, Pop., Bayboro.

Pasquotank—J. H. Parker, Pop., Hertford.

Pender—Gibson James, Dem., Maple Hill.

Perquimans—J. H. Parker, Pop., Hertford.

Person—Jno. S. Cunningham, Dem., Cunningham.

Pitt—Slade Chapman, Pop., Coxville; E. V. Cox, Rep., Coxville.

Polk—Grayson Alredge, Rep., Mill Springs.

Randolph—J. J. White, Pop., Trinity; J. M. Allen, Rep., Ralph.

Richmond—Y. C. Morton, Pop., Rockingham; Claudius Dockery, Rep., Rockingham.

Robeson—D. E. McBride, Pop., Mill Prong; W. J. Currie, Rep., Maxton.

Rockingham— A. E. Walters, Dem., Reidsville ; P. P. Foster, Pop., Oregon.

Rowan—J. W. McKenzie, Dem., Salisbury; Walter Murphy, Dem , Salisbury.

Rutherford—Lindsey Purgason, Pop., Logan's Store.

Sampson—C. H. Johnson, Pop., Ingold; R. M. Crumpler, Pop., Clinton.

Stanly — E. F. Eddins, Dem., Farmerville.

Stokes—R. J. Petree, Rep., Danbury.

Surry—J. M. Brower, Rep., Mt. Airy.

Swain — J. H. Cathey, Dem., Brison City.

Transylvania—A.E. Aiken, Rep., Brevard.

Tyrell—Dr. Ab. Alexander, Rep., Columbia.

Union—J. M. Price, Pop., Price's Mill.

Vance—M. M Peace, Rep., Henderson.

Wake—J. M. Ferrell, Pop., Eagle Rock; J. P. H. Adams, Rep., Cary; Jas. H. Young, Rep., Raleigh.

Warren—C. A. Cook, Rep., Warrenton.

Watauga—Thos. Bingham, Rep., Amantha.

Washington—L. N. C. Spruill, Rep., Mackey's Ferry.

Wayne—Dr. J. E. Person, Pop., Pikeville; T. B. Parker, Dem., Goldsboro.

Wilkes—J. Q. A. Bryan, Rep., Trap Hill; Chas. H. Somers, Rep., Wilkesboro.

Wilson—B. T. Person, Pop., Wilson.

Yadkin — J. C. Pinnix, Rep., Malee.

Yancey—C. L. McPeters, Dem., Bald Creek.

NOTE.—There are two negroes in the Senate and nine in the House, to-wit:

Senate—Person, 5th District, and Henderson, 11th District.

House—Dancy and Bryant of Edgecombe, Crews of Granville, Arrington and Harris of Halifax, Howe of New Hanover, Rawls of Northampton, Peace of Vance, and Young of Wake.

Crews' seat contested by A. J. Fields, and Young's seat contested by N. B. Broughton.

A SHORT.

A stingy fellow—'tis no matter who—
Had once upon a time some work to do;
He told a negro man named Sam, I think,
That if he'd do his job he'd give him drink
Such as could not in any place be sold,
For it was then exactly ten years old.
The work is done; the miser gives the dram.
"How old do you call this. Massa?" says poor Sam;
"Ten years, exactly." "Ten years!" in a rage
Says Sam; "he be d——n little of his age."

DURHAM ALMANAC. 47

INSURANCE BUSINESS.

There are 119 insurance companies doing business in North Carolina—29 life, 10 accident, 11 co-operative life, 4 guarantee, fidelity and trust companies, and 65 fire and marine. Of all these, only 6 are North Carolina companies, and it is safe to say that 95 per cent of all the money paid out on insurance premiums by our people finds its way beyond the borders of the State. *This ought not to be.*

BLIND ALEX'S WONDERFUL MEMORY.

Blind Alex, who lived in Stirling, Scotland, from 1830 to about 1840, had the most wonderful memory of which any account has ever been recorded. He was familiarly known as "The Complete Concordance," on account of the fact that he knew the entire Old and New Testaments "by heart." He was tested a half dozen or more different times before the Scottish Society of Advanced Learning, and always succeeded in convincing the professors that he was all that had been claimed for him. If any sentence in the entire Bible was repeated to him, he would instantly name chapter and verse; or if the book, chapter and verse were named, he could give the exact words of the quotation.

A WELL-TO-DO PEOPLE.

The Osage Indians are 1,500 strong. In addition to a large reservation with houses and cattle, they have to their credit in the U. S. Treasury over $8,000,000, on which they receive every quarter $100,000 in cash, or an average per capita of $22.22 per month.

BEAUTIFUL SHADE TREES AT 7.35 A. M. BECOME NEWSPAPERS AT 10.00 O'CLOCK.

A trial was recently made in Austria to decide how short a space of time living trees could be converted into newspapers. At Elsenthal, at 7.35 A. M., three trees were sawn down; at 9.34, the wood having been stripped of bark, cut up and converted into pulp, became paper, and passed from the factory to the press, from whence the first printed and folded copy was issued at 10 o'clock.

Reliable and Satisfactory ! **Blackwell's Durham Tobacco.**

THE MAN to be pitied above all others in this world, is he who has nothing else but money.

THE BIGGEST LENS in the world has just been completed for the Observatory at Lake Geneva, Wisconsin. It is 41¾ inches in diameter, and weighs 205 pounds. It took two and a half years to make it, at a cost of $100,000.

WHY IS IT?

Some find work where some find rest,
  And so the weary world goes on.
I sometimes wonder which is best—
  The answer comes when life is gone.

Some eyes sleep when some eyes wake,
  And so the dreary night hours go.
Some hearts beat where some hearts break—
  I often wonder why 'tis so.

Some will faint where some will fight;
  Some love the tent while some the field.
I often wonder who are right—
  The ones who strive or those who yield.

Some hands fold where other hands
  Are lifted bravely in the strife—
And so through ages and through lands
  Move on the two extremes of life.

Some feet halt where some feet tread
  In tireless march a thorny way;
Some struggle on where some have fled,
  Some seek when others shun the fray.

Some swords rust where others clash,
  Some fall back where some move on;
Some flags furl where others flash
  Until the battle has been won.

Some sleep on while others keep
  The vigils of the true and brave;
They will not rest till roses creep
  Around their names above a grave.
                              —*Father Ryan.*

A CHEAP PLACE TO RAISE KIDS.

It is said that it costs less than $3 to raise a child to maturity in Egypt.

The Man in the Moon

would be happier if he could have a supply of

Cool
Fragrant
and Soothing

Blackwell's Bull Durham
Smoking Tobacco

For over twenty-five years the standard smoking tobacco of the world.

To-day More Popular than Ever.

To have a good smoke anytime and everytime it is only necessary to get Bull Durham.   It is all good and always good.

BLACKWELL'S DURHAM TOBACCO CO.,
DURHAM, N. C.

FIRST NATIONAL BANK OF DURHAM,

Corner Main and Corcoran Streets,

DURHAM, N. C.

Capital Stock, - - -	$150,000.00
Stockholders' Liabilities, -	150,000.00
Depositors' Security, - -	300,000.00
Surplus and Undivided Profits	22,475.41

BANKING IN ALL ITS BRANCHES.

Liberal Inducements for Deposits from Banks, Corporations,
Business Houses and Individuals. Our Facilities for
making Collections on all points throughout the State are the best.

ALL RETURNS MADE PROMPTLY.

PRINCIPAL CORRESPONDENTS:

United States National Bank, New York City, N. Y.
National Bank Republic, New York City, N. Y.
National Park Bank, New York City, N. Y.
Manufacturers' National Bank, Philadelphia, Pa.
National Union Bank, Baltimore, Md.
State Bank of Virginia, Richmond, Va,
Norfolk National Bank, Norfolk, Va.
National Bank of Raleigh, Raleigh, N. C.
Commercial National Bank, Charlotte, N. C.

Our Discount Rate is 8 Per Cent. to Everybody.

OFFICERS

J. S. CARR, President.   L. D. HEARTT, Cashier.
J. M. WHITTED, Teller.   W. J. HOLLOWAY, Bookkeeper.

DIRECTORS:

J. S. CARR,	J. W. SMITH,	P. W. VAUGHAN,
J. T. MALLORY,	J. S. MANNING,	V. S. BRYANT.
	JAS. A. BRYAN	

THE FIDELITY BANK,

DURHAM, N. C.

Capital,	-	-	-	$100,000.
Surplus,	-	-	-	30,000.

COUNTY AND CITY DEPOSITORY.

OFFICERS:

B. N. Duke, President.

A. E. Lloyd, Vice-President.

Jno. F. Wily, Cashier.

W. W. Whitted, Teller.

DIRECTORS:

B. N. Duke,	W. H. Proctor,	S. R. Carrington,
Geo. W. Watts,	A. E. Lloyd,	John F. Wily,
F. L. Fuller,	Samuel Kramer,	W. H. Branson,
	W. Duke.	

This Bank extends every accomodation to its customers consistent with Sound Banking.

We only want the business of responsible people.

INTEREST PAID ON DEPOSITS.

The *Chesapeake* 🌿

And *Ohio Route.*

✗ ✗ ✗

THE SHORTEST AND QUICKEST TIME

FROM NORTH CAROLINA TO

Cincinnati, O., Louisville, Ky., Chicago, Ills., St. Louis, Mo.,
and all Points in the West.

✗ ✗ ✗

RATES ALWAYS AS LOW AS BY ANY OTHER ROUTE.

✗ ✗ ✗

Superb Train Service, Unsurpassed by any Other Line. Electric-
Lighted and Steam-Heated. Vestibuled Coaches and
Pullman's Finest and Newest Sleeping Cars.
Meals Served on Dining Cars on all
Through Trains.

✗ ✗ ✗

NO EXTRA CHARGE FOR SUPERIOR SERVICE.

✗ ✗ ✗

If you wish to go to the West, ask your nearest Coupon
Ticket Agent for Rates and Tickets via. C. & O. Route, or address
J. C. Dame, T. P. A. C. & O. Ry., Richmond, Va.

✗ ✗ ✗

H. W. FULLER,   JNO. D. POTTS,
  G. P. A. C. & O. Ry.,   A. G. P. A. C. &. O. Ry.,
    Washington, D. C.   Richmond, Va.

PEACE
INSTITUTE,

RALEIGH, N. C.

✻ ✻ ✻

A Select School for young Ladies.
Complete in its Appointments and
Thorough in Scholarship.

✻ ✻ ✻

ART DEPARTMENT

Is in charge of an honor graduate of the School of Designs at
Philadelphia.

✻ ✻ ✻

Two Directors of Music—one a graduate
of Leipsic, the other of Boston.
Four Assistants in Music.
Twenty-one Officers and Teachers.
Special Attention to Physical Culture.
Good fare.

Careful attention to Physical Condition.
Medical Attention Furnished.
Also a Special Nurse for those who may
be taken sick.

For catalogue and full information, address the Principal,

JAMES DINWIDDIE, M. A.,

(University of Va,)

THE STYRON FENCE CO.

Office: No. 141 Water Street, NORFOLK, VA.

Factory : HUNTERSVILLE, VA.

Manufacturers of

Styron Fence and Gates and the Celebrated O. G. Poultry Fences.

—DEALERS IN—

RED CEDAR POSTS, FENCE SUPPLIES, ETC.

Send for Circulars and Price List.

DESCRIPTION: The Styron Fence is composed of White Cedar Pickets and Galvanized Bessemer Steel Fence Wire. The Pickets are woven between wires, as shown in above cut. The wires begin three inches from the bottom, and run every ten inches apart to within three inches of the top. The pickets are spear pointed. The fence is manufactured in rolls of 50, 75 and 100 lineal feet, and weighs from 125 to 250 pounds per roll. On a four-foot fence there are five cables of two wires each, which gives the fence a resistance of about 8,050 pounds.

☞ *One good, reliable agent wanted in every town in the South.*

N. A. RAMSEY, Agent,
DURHAM, N. C.

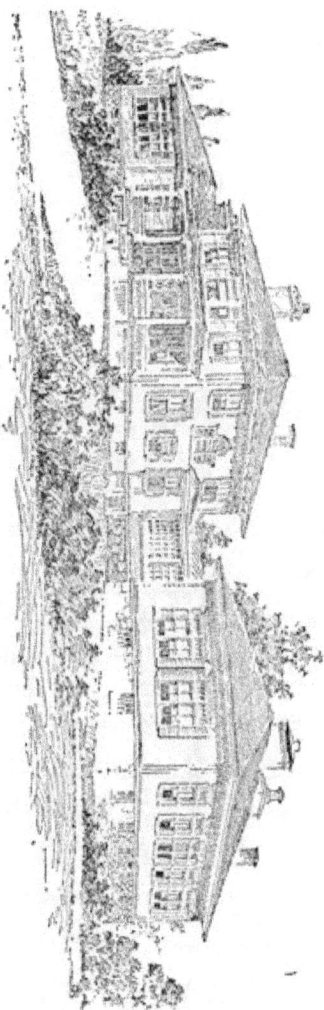

WATTS HOSPITAL, DURHAM, N. C.

DEDICATED 21ST FEBRUARY, 1895.

DONATED TO THE TOWN OF DURHAM BY GEORGE W. WATTS, TOGETHER WITH AN ENDOWMENT FUND OF $20,000.

OCCONEECHEE FARM. 266 PRIZES WITH 2 MEDALS.

J.S.C.

BREEDERS OF

STANDARD AND THOROUGHBRED HORSES. FINE JERSEY AND BLACK ESSEX HOGS. PRIZE WINNING POULTRY OF ALL KINDS. BRONZE TURKEYS. PEKIN DUCKS. PEA FOWLS.

FAMILIES SUPPLIED ON YEAR ROUND CONTRACTS WITH GILT EDGE OCCONEECHEE BUTTER.

WRITE FOR CATALOGUE: ADDRESS OCCONEECHEE FARM DURHAM, N.C.

* 9 7 8 3 3 3 7 3 3 4 6 0 4 *